THE MASTER OF MRS. CHILVERS—AN IMPROBABLE COMEDY

By

Jerome K. Jerome

British Library Cataloguing-in-Publication Data
A catalogue record for this book is available from the
British Library

Jerome K. Jerome

Jerome Klapka Jerome was born in Walsall, England in 1859. Both his parents died while he was in his early teens, and he was forced to quit school to support himself. Jerome worked for a number of years collecting coal along railway tracks, before trying his hand at acting, journalism, teaching and soliciting. At long last, in 1885, he had some success with *On the Stage – and Off*, a comic memoir of his experiences with an acting troupe. Jerome produced a number of essays over the following years, and married in 1888, spending the honeymoon in "a little boat" on the Thames.

In 1889, Jerome published his most successful and best-remembered work, *Three Men in a Boat*. Featuring himself and two of his friends encountering humorous situations while floating down the Thames in a small boat, the book was an instant success, and has never been out of print. In fact, its popularity was such that the number of registered Thames boats went up fifty percent in the year following its publication. With the financial security provided by *Three Men in a Boat*, Jerome was able to dedicate himself fully to writing, producing eleven more novels and a number of anthologies of short fiction.

In 1926, Jerome published his autobiography, *My Life and Times*. He died a year later, aged 68.

THE FIRST ACT
SCENE: Drawing-room, 91, Russell Square.
TIME: 3 p.m.

THE SECOND ACT
SCENE: Liberal Committee Room, East India Dock
Road.
TIME: 5 p.m.

THE THIRD ACT
SCENE: The Town Hall, East Poplar.
TIME: 10 p.m.

THE FOURTH ACT
SCENE: Russell Square
TIME: Midnight

THE CAST OF "THE MASTER OF MRS. CHILVERS"

AS IT WAS PRODUCED AT THE ROYALTY THEATRE, LONDON, ON APRIL 26TH, 1911, UNDER THE MANAGEMENT OF MESSRS. VEDRENNE & EADIE.

Lady Mogton .... Mary Rorke

Annys Chilvers .... Lena Ashwell

Phoebe Mogton .... Ethel Dane

Janet Blake .... Gillian Scaife

Mrs. Mountcalm Villiers ..... Sarah Brooke

Elizabeth Spender .... Auriol Lee

Rose Merton .... Esme Beringer

Mrs. Chinn .... Sydney Fairbrother

Geoffrey Chilvers, M.P. .... Dennis Eadie

Dorian St. Herbert .... Leon Quartermaine

Ben Lamb, M.P. .... A. E. Benedict

William Gordon .... Edmund Gwenn

Sigsby .... Michael Sherbrooke

Hake .... H. B. Tabberer

Mr. Peekin .... Gerald Mirrielees

Mr. Hopper .... Stanley Logan

Mrs. Peekin .... Rowena Jerome

Miss Borlasse .... Cathleen Nesbitt

Miss Ricketts .... Hetta Bartlett

CHARACTERS IN THE PLAY

GEOFFREY CHILVERS, M.P. [President Men's League for the Extension of the Franchise to Women] A loving husband, and (would-be) affectionate father. Like many other good men, he is in sympathy with the Woman's Movement: "not thinking it is coming in his time."

ANNYS CHILVERS [nee Mogton, Hon. Sec. Women's Parliamentary Franchise League] A loving wife, and (would-be) affection mother. Many thousands of years have gone to her making. A generation ago, she would have been the ideal woman: the ideal helpmeet. But new ideas are stirring in her blood, a new ideal of womanhood is forcing itself upon her.

LADY MOGTON [President W.P.F.L.]

She knows she would be of more use in Parliament than many of the men who are there; is naturally annoyed at the Law's stupidity in keeping her out.

PHOEBE MOGTON [Org. Sec. W.P.F.L.] The new girl, thinking more of politics than of boys. But that will probably pass.

JANET BLAKE [Jt. Org. Sec. W.P.F.L.] She dreams of a new heaven and a new earth when woman has the vote.

MRS. MOUNTCALM VILLIERS [Vice-President W.P.F.L.] She was getting tired of flirting. The Woman's Movement has arrived just at the right moment.

ELIZABETH SPENDER [Hons. Treas. W.P.F.L.] She sees woman everywhere the slave of man: now pampered, now beaten, but ever the slave. She can see no hope of freedom but through warfare.

MRS. CHINN A mother.

JAWBONES A bill-poster. Movements that do not fit in with the essentials of life on thirty shillings a week have no message so far as Jawbones is concerned.

GINGER Whose proper name is Rose Merton, and who has to reconcile herself to the fact that so far as her class is concerned the primaeval laws still run.

DORIAN ST. HERBERT [Hon. Sec. M.L.E.F.W.] He is interested in all things, the Woman's Movement included.

BEN LAMB, M.P. As a student of woman, he admits to being in the infants' class.

SIGSBY An Election Agent. He thinks the modern woman suffers from over-indulgence. He would recommend to her the teachings of St. Paul.

HAKE A butler. He does not see how to avoid his wife being practically a domestic servant without wages.

A DEPUTATION It consists of two men and three women. Superior people would call them Cranks. But Cranks have been of some service to the world, and the use of superior people is still to be discovered.

THE FIRST ACT

SCENE:- Drawing-room, 91, Russell Square.

TIME:- Afternoon.

[MRS. ELIZABETH SPENDER sits near the fire, reading a book. She is a tall, thin woman, with passionate eyes, set in an oval face of olive complexion; the features are regular and severe; her massive dark hair is almost primly arranged. She wears a tailor-made costume, surmounted by a plain black hat. The door opens and PHOEBE enters, shown in by HAKE, the butler, a thin, ascetic- looking man of about thirty, with prematurely grey hair. PHOEBE MOGTON is of the Fluffy Ruffles type, petite, with a retrousse nose, remarkably bright eyes, and a quantity of fluffy light hair, somewhat untidily arranged. She is fashionably dressed in the fussy, flyaway style. ELIZABETH looks up; the two young women shake hands.]

PHOEBE Good woman. 'Tisn't three o'clock yet, is it?

ELIZABETH About five minutes to.

PHOEBE Annys is on her way. I just caught her in time. [To HAKE.] Put a table and six chairs. Give mamma a hammer and a cushion at her back.

HAKE A hammer, miss?

PHOEBE A chairman's hammer. Haven't you got one?

HAKE I'm afraid not, miss. Would a gravy spoon do?

PHOEBE [To ELIZABETH, after expression of disgust.] Fancy a house without a chairman's hammer! [To HAKE.] See that there's something. Did your wife go to the meeting last night?

HAKE [He is arranging furniture according to instructions.] I'm not quite sure, miss. I gave her the evening out.

PHOEBE "Gave her the evening out"!

ELIZABETH We are speaking of your wife, man, not your servant.

HAKE Yes, miss. You see, we don't keep servants in our class.
Somebody's got to put the children to bed.

ELIZABETH Why not the man—occasionally?

HAKE Well, you see, miss, in my case, I rarely getting home much before midnight, it would make it so late. Yesterday being my night off, things fitted in, so to speak. Will there be any writing, miss?

PHOEBE Yes. See that there's plenty of blotting-paper. [To ELIZABETH.] Mamma always splashes so.

HAKE Yes, miss. [He goes out.]

ELIZABETH Did you ever hear anything more delightfully naive? He "gave" her the evening out. That's how they think of us—as their servants. The gentleman hasn't the courage to be straightforward about it. The butler blurts out the truth. Why are we meeting here instead of at our own place?

PHOEBE For secrecy, I expect. Too many gasbags always about the office. I fancy—I'm not quite sure—that mamma's got a new idea.

ELIZABETH Leading to Holloway?

PHOEBE Well, most roads lead there.

ELIZABETH And end there—so far as I can see.

PHOEBE You're too impatient.

ELIZABETH It's what our friends have been telling us—for the last fifty years.

PHOEBE Look here, if it was only the usual sort of thing mamma wouldn't want it kept secret. I'm inclined to think it's a new departure altogether.

[The door opens. There enters JANET BLAKE, followed by HAKE, who proceeds with his work. JANET BLAKE is a slight, fragile-looking creature, her great dark eyes—

the eyes of a fanatic—emphasise the pallor of her childish face. She is shabbily dressed; a plain, uninteresting girl until she smiles, and then her face becomes quite beautiful. PHOEBE darts to meet her.] Good girl. Was afraid—I say, you're wet through.

JANET It was only a shower. The 'buses were all full. I had to ride outside.

PHOEBE Silly kid, why didn't you take a cab?

JANET I've been reckoning it up. I've been half over London chasing Mrs. Mountcalm-Villiers. Cabs would have come, at the very least, to twelve-and-six.

PHOEBE Well -

JANET [To ELIZABETH.] Well—I want you to put me down as a contributor for twelve-and-six. [She smiles.] It's the only way I can give.

PHOEBE [She is taking off JANET'S cloak; throws it to HAKE.] Have this put somewhere to dry. [She pushes JANET to the fire.] Get near the fire. You're as cold as ice.

ELIZABETH All the seats inside, I suppose, occupied by the chivalrous sex.

JANET Oh, there was one young fellow offered to give me up his place, but I wouldn't let him. You see, we're claiming equality. [Smiles.]

ELIZABETH And are being granted it—in every direction where it works to the convenience of man.

PHOEBE [Laughs.] Is she coming—the Villiers woman?

JANET Yes. I ran her down at last—at her dress-maker's. She made an awful fuss about it, but I wouldn't leave till she'd promised. Tell me, it's something quite important, isn't it?

PHOEBE I don't know anything, except that I had an urgent telegram from mamma this morning to call a meeting of the entire Council here at three o'clock. She's coming up from Manchester on purpose. [To HAKE.] Mrs. Chilvers hasn't returned yet, has she?

HAKE Not yet, miss. Shall I telephone -

PHOEBE [Shakes her head.] No; it's all right. I have seen her. Let her know we are here the moment she comes in.

HAKE Yes, miss. [He has finished the arrangements. The table has been placed in the centre of the room, six chairs round it, one of them being a large armchair. He has placed writing materials and a large silver gravy spoon. He is going.]

PHOEBE Why aren't you sure your wife wasn't at the meeting last night? Didn't she say anything?

HAKE Well, miss, unfortunately, just as she was starting, Mrs. Comerford—that's the wife of the party that keeps the shop downstairs—looked in with an order for the theatre.

PHOEBE Oh!

HAKE So I thought it best to ask no questions.

PHOEBE Thank you.

HAKE Thank you, miss. [He goes out.]

ELIZABETH Can nothing be done to rouse the working-class woman out of her apathy?

PHOEBE Well, if you ask me, I think a good deal has been done.

ELIZABETH Oh, what's the use of our deceiving ourselves? The great mass are utterly indifferent.

JANET [She is seated in an easy-chair near the fire.] I was talking to a woman only yesterday—in Bethnal Green. She keeps a husband and three children by taking in washing. "Lord, miss," she laughed, "what would we do with the vote if we did have it? Only one thing more to give to the men."

PHOEBE That's rather good.

ELIZABETH The curse of it is that it's true. Why should they put themselves out merely that one man instead of another should dictate their laws to them?

PHOEBE My dear girl, precisely the same argument was used against the Second Reform Bill. What earthly difference could it make to the working men whether Tory Squire or Liberal capitalist ruled over them? That was in 1868. To-day, fifty-four Labour Members sit in Parliament. At the next election they will hold the balance.

ELIZABETH Ah, if we could only hold out THAT sort of hope to them!

[ANNYS enters. She is in outdoor costume. She kisses PHOEBE, shakes hands with the other two. ANNYS's age is about twenty-five. She is a beautiful, spiritual-looking creature, tall and graceful, with a manner that is at the same time appealing and commanding. Her voice is soft and caressing, but capable of expressing all the emotions. Her likeness to her younger sister PHOEBE is of the slightest: the colouring is the same, and the eyes that can flash, but there the similarity ends. She is simply but well dressed. Her soft hair makes a quiet but wonderfully effective frame to her face.]

ANNYS [She is taking off her outdoor things.] Hope I'm not late. I had to look in at Caxton House. Why are we holding it here?

PHOEBE Mamma's instructions. Can't tell you anything more except that I gather the matter's important, and is to be kept secret.

ANNYS Mamma isn't here, is she?

PHOEBE [Shakes her head.] Reaches St. Pancras at two-forty.
[Looks at her watch.] Train's late, I expect.

[HAKE has entered.]

ANNYS [She hands HAKE her hat and coat.] Have something ready in case Lady Mogton hasn't lunched. Is your master in?

HAKE A messenger came for him soon after you left, ma'am. I was to tell you he would most likely be dining at the House.

ANNYS Thank you.

[HAKE goes out.]

ANNYS [To ELIZABETH.] I so want you to meet Geoffrey. He'll alter your opinion of men.

ELIZABETH My opinion of men has been altered once or twice—each time for the worse.

ANNYS Why do you dislike men?

ELIZABETH [With a short laugh.] Why does the slave dislike the slave-owner?

PHOEBE Oh, come off the perch. You spend five thousand a year provided for you by a husband that you only see on Sundays. We'd all be slaves at that price.

ELIZABETH The chains have always been stretched for the few. My sympathies are with my class.

ANNYS But men like Geoffrey—men who are devoting their whole time and energy to furthering our cause; what can you have to say against them?

ELIZABETH Simply that they don't know what they're doing. The French Revolution was nursed in the salons of the French nobility. When the true meaning of the woman's movement is understood we shall have to get on without the male sympathiser.

[A pause.]

ANNYS What do you understand is the true meaning of the woman's movement?

ELIZABETH The dragging down of man from his position of supremacy. What else can it mean?

ANNYS Something much better. The lifting up of woman to be his partner.

ELIZABETH My dear Annys, the men who to-day are advocating votes for women are doing so in the hope of securing obedient supporters for their own political schemes. In New Zealand the working man brings his female relations in a van to the poll, and sees to it that they vote in accordance with his orders. When man once grasps the fact that woman is not going to be his henchman, but his rival, men and women will face one another as enemies.

[The door opens. HAKE announces LADY MOGTON and DORIAN ST. HERBERT. LADY MOGTON is a large, strong-featured woman, with a naturally loud voice. She is dressed with studied carelessness. DORIAN ST. HERBERT, K.C., is a tall, thin man, about thirty. He is elegantly, almost dandily dressed.]

ANNYS [Kissing her mother.] Have you had lunch?

LADY MOGTON In the train.

PHOEBE [Who has also kissed her mother and shaken hands with ST. HERBERT.] We are all here except Villiers. She's coming. Did you have a good meeting?

LADY MOGTON Fairly. Some young fool had chained himself to a pillar and thrown the key out of window.

PHOEBE What did you do?

LADY MOGTON Tied a sack over his head and left him there.

[She turns aside for a moment to talk to ST. HERBERT, who has taken some papers from his despatch-box.]

ANNYS [To ELIZABETH.] We must finish out our talk some other time. You are quite wrong.

ELIZABETH Perhaps.

LADY MOGTON We had better begin. I have only got half an hour.

JANET I saw Mrs. Villiers. She promised she'd come.

LADY MOGTON You should have told her we were going to be photographed. Then she'd have been punctual. [She has taken her seat at the table. ST. HERBERT at her right.] Better put another chair in case she does turn up.

JANET [Does so.] Shall I take any notes?

LADY MOGTON No. [To ANNYS.] Give instructions that we are not to be interrupted for anything. [ANNYS rings bell.]

ST. HERBERT [He turns to PHOEBE, on his right.] Have you heard the latest?

There was an old man of Hong Kong,
Whose language was terribly strong.

[Enter HAKE. He brings a bottle and glass, which he places.]

ANNYS Oh, Hake, please, don't let us be interrupted for anything. If Mrs. Mountcalm-Villiers comes, show her up. But nobody else.

HAKE Yes, ma'am.

ST. HERBERT [Continuing.]

It wasn't the words
That frightened the birds,
'Twas the 'orrible double-entendre.

LADY MOGTON [Who has sat waiting in grim silence.] Have you finished?

ST. HERBERT Quite finished.

LADY MOGTON Thank you. [She raps for silence.] You will understand, please, all, that this is a private meeting of the Council. Nothing that transpires is to be allowed to leak out. [There is a murmur.] Silence, please, for Mr. St. Herbert.

ST. HERBERT Before we begin, I should like to remind you, ladies, that you are, all of you, persons mentally deficient -

[The door opens. MRS. MOUNTCALM-VILLIERS enters, announced by HAKE. She is a showily-dressed, flamboyant lady.]

[HAKE goes out.]

MRS. MOUNTCALM-VILLIERS I AM so sorry. I have only just this minute—[She catches sight of ST. HERBERT.] You naughty creature, why weren't you at my meeting last night? The Rajah came with both his wives. We've elected them, all three, honorary members.

LADY MOGTON Do you mind sitting down?

MRS. MOUNTCALM-VILLIERS Here, dear? [She takes the vacant chair.] So nice of you. I read about your meeting. What a clever idea!

LADY MOGTON [Cuts her short.] Yes. We are here to consider a very important matter. By way of commencement Mr. St. Herbert has just reminded us that in the eye of the law all women are imbeciles.

MRS. MOUNTCALM-VILLIERS I know, dear. Isn't it shocking?

ST. HERBERT Deplorable; but of course not your fault. I mention it because of its importance to the present matter. Under Clause A of the Act for the Better Regulation, &c., &c., all persons "mentally deficient" are debarred from becoming members of Parliament. The classification has been held to include idiots, infants, and women.

[An interruption. LADY MOGTON hammers.]

Bearing this carefully in mind, we proceed. [He refers to his notes.] Two years ago a bye-election took place for the South-west division of Belfast.

MRS. MOUNTCALM-VILLIERS My dear, may I? It has just occurred to me. Why do we never go to Ireland?

LADY MOGTON For various sufficient reasons.

MRS. MOUNTCALM-VILLIERS So many of the Irish members have expressed themselves quite sympathetically.

LADY MOGTON We wish them to continue to do so. [Turns to ST. HERBERT.] I'm sorry.

ST. HERBERT A leader of the Orange Party was opposed by a Nationalist, and the proceedings promised to be lively. They promised for a while to be still livelier, owing to the nomination at the last moment of the local lunatic.

PHOEBE [To ANNYS.] This is where we come in.

ST. HERBERT There is always a local lunatic, who, if harmless, is generally a popular character. James Washington McCaw appears to have been a particularly cheerful specimen. One of his eccentricities was to always have a skipping-rope in his pocket; wherever the traffic allowed it, he would go through the streets skipping. He said it kept him warm. Another of his tricks was to let off fireworks from the roof of his house whenever he heard of the death of anybody of importance. The Returning Officer refused his nomination—which, so far as his nominators were concerned, was intended only as a joke—on the grounds of his being by common report a person of unsound mind. And there, so far as South-west Belfast was concerned, the matter ended.

PHOEBE Pity.

ST. HERBERT But not so far as the Returning Officer was concerned. McCaw appears to have been a lunatic possessed of means, imbued with all an Irishman's love of litigation. He at once brought an action against the Returning Officer, his contention being that his mental state was a private matter, of which the Returning Officer was not the person to judge.

PHOEBE He wasn't a lunatic all over.

ST. HERBERT We none of us are. The case went from court to court. In every instance the decision was in favour of the Returning Officer. Until it reached the House of Lords. The decision was given yesterday afternoon—in favour of the man McCaw.

ELIZABETH Then lunatics, at all events, are not debarred from going to the poll.

ST. HERBERT The "mentally deficient" are no longer debarred from going to the poll.

ELIZABETH What grounds were given for the decision?

ST. HERBERT [He refers again to his notes.] A Returning Officer can only deal with objections arising out of the nomination paper. He has no jurisdiction to go behind a nomination paper and constitute himself a court of inquiry as to the fitness or unfitness of a candidate.

PHOEBE Good old House of Lords!

[LADY MOGTON hammers.]

ELIZABETH But I thought it was part of the Returning Officer's duty to inquire into objections, that a special time was appointed to deal with them.

ST. HERBERT He will still be required to take cognisance of any informality in the nomination paper or papers. Beyond that, this decision relieves him of all further responsibility.

JANET But this gives us everything.

ST. HERBERT It depends upon what you call everything. It gives a woman the right to go to the poll—a right which, as a matter of fact, she has always possessed.

PHOEBE Then why did the Returning Officer for Camberwell in 1885 -

ST. HERBERT Because he did not know the law. And Miss Helen Taylor had not the means possessed by our friend McCaw to teach it to him.

ANNYS [Rises. She goes to the centre of the room.]

LADY MOGTON Where are you going?

ANNYS [She turns; there are tears in her eyes. The question seems to recall her to herself.] Nowhere. I am so sorry. I can't help it. It seems to me to mean so much. It gives us the right to go before the people—to plead to them, not for ourselves, for them. [Again she seems to lose consciousness of those at the table, of the room.] To the men we will say: "Will you not trust us? Is it harm we have ever done you? Have we not suffered for you and with you? Were we not sent into the world to be your helpmeet? Are not the children ours as well as yours? Shall we not work together to shape the world where they must dwell? Is it only the mother-voice that shall not be heard in your councils? Is it only the mother-hand that shall not help to guide?" To the women we will say: "Tell them—tell them it is from no love of ourselves that we come from our sheltered homes into the street. It is to give, not to get—to mingle with the sterner judgments of men the deeper truths that God, through pain, has taught to women—to mingle with man's justice woman's pity, till there shall arise the perfect law—not made of man nor woman, but of both, each bringing what the other lacks." And they will listen to us. Till now it has seemed to them that we were clamouring only for selfish ends. They have not understood. We shall speak to them of common purposes, use the language of fellow-citizens. They will see that we are worthy of the place we claim. They will welcome us as helpers in a common cause. They -

[She turns—the present comes back to her.]

LADY MOGTON [After a pause.] The business [she dwells severely on the word] before the meeting -

ANNYS [She resents herself meekly. Apologising generally.] I must learn to control myself.

LADY MOGTON [Who has waited.]—is McCaw versus Potts. Its bearing upon the movement for the extension of the franchise to women. My own view I venture to submit in the form of a resolution. [She takes up a paper on which she has been writing.] As follows: That the Council of the Woman's Parliamentary

Franchise League, having regard to the decision of the House of Lords in McCaw v. Potts -

ST. HERBERT [Looking over.] Two t's.

LADY MOGTON —resolves to bring forward a woman candidate to contest the next bye-election. [Suddenly to MRS. MOUNTCALM- VILLIERS, who is chattering.] Do you agree or disagree?

MRS. MOUNTCALM-VILLIERS My dear! How can you ask? Of course we all agree. [To Elizabeth.] You agree, don't you?

ELIZABETH Of course, even if elected, she would not be allowed to take her seat.

PHOEBE How do you know? Nothing more full of surprises than English law.

LADY MOGTON At the present stage I regard that point as immaterial. What I am thinking of is the advertisement. A female candidate upon the platform will concentrate the whole attention of the country on our movement.

ST. HERBERT It might even be prudent—until you have got the vote- -to keep it dark that you will soon be proceeding to the next inevitable step.

ELIZABETH You think even man could be so easily deceived!

ST. HERBERT Man has had so much practice in being deceived. It comes naturally to him.

ELIZABETH Poor devil!

LADY MOGTON The only question remaining to be discussed is the candidate.

ANNYS Is there not danger that between now and the next bye- election the Government may, having regard to this case, bring in a bill to stop women candidates from going to the poll?

ST. HERBERT I have thought of that. Fortunately, the case seems to have attracted very little attention. If a bye-election occurred soon there would hardly be time.

LADY MOGTON It must be the very next one that does occur—wherever it is.

JANET I am sure that in the East End we should have a chance.

PHOEBE Great Scott! Just think. If we were to win it!

ST. HERBERT If you could get a straight fight against a Liberal I believe you would.

ANNYS Why is the Government so unpopular?

ST. HERBERT Well, take the weather alone—twelve degrees of frost again last night.

JANET In St. George's Road the sewer has burst. The water is in the rooms where the children are sleeping. [She clenches her hands.]

MRS. MOUNTCALM-VILLIERS [She shakes her head.] Something ought really to be done.

LADY MOGTON Has anybody any suggestion to make?—as regards the candidate. There's no advantage in going outside. It will have to be one of ourselves.

MRS. MOUNTCALM-VILLIERS Won't you, dear?

LADY MOGTON I shall be better employed organising. My own feeling is that it ought to be Annys. [To ST. HERBERT.] What do you think?

ST. HERBERT Undoubtedly.

ANNYS I'd rather not.

LADY MOGTON It's not a question of liking. It's a question of duty. For this occasion we shall be appealing to the male voter. Our candidate must be a woman popular with men. The choice is somewhat limited.

ELIZABETH No one will put up so good a fight as you.

ANNYS Will you give me till this evening?

LADY MOGTON What for?

ANNYS I should like to consult Geoffrey.

LADY MOGTON You think he would object?

ANNYS [A little doubtfully.] No. But we have always talked everything over together.

LADY MOGTON Absurd! He's one of our staunchest supporters. Of course he'll be delighted.

ELIZABETH I think the thing ought to be settled at once.

LADY MOGTON It must be. I have to return to Manchester to-night. We shall have to get to work immediately.

ST. HERBERT Geoffrey will surely take it as a compliment.

JANET Don't you feel that woman, all over the world, is calling to you?

ANNYS It isn't that. I'm not trying to shirk it. I merely thought that if there had been time—of course, if you really think -

LADY MOGTON You consent?

ANNYS Yes. If it's everybody's wish.

LADY MOGTON That's settled.

PHOEBE [She springs up, waving a handkerchief.] Chilvers for ever!

JANET [Rises.] God bless you!

MRS. MOUNTCALM-VILLIERS [Clapping her hands.] Now we shan't be long!

LADY MOGTON [Hammers.] Order, please!

[The three subside.]

This is serious business. The next step is, of course -

[The door opens; GEOFFREY enters. He is a youngish-looking man of three or four and thirty. LADY MOGTON, at the sound of the door, turns. ST. HERBERT rises. There is a pause.]

LADY MOGTON We've been talking about you. We must apologise for turning your drawing-room -

GEOFFREY My dear mother-in-law, it is Providence. [He kisses her.] There is no one I was more longing to see.

ANNYS [She has risen.] Hake told me you would be dining at the House.

GEOFFREY [He comes to her, kisses her, he is in a state of suppressed excitement.] I shall be. I came back to bring you some news.

PHOEBE We've got some news for you. Have you heard -

GEOFFREY [He stays her.] May I claim man's privilege for the first word? It is news, I am sure, you will all be delighted to hear. A friend of yours has been appointed to an office where—it is quite possible—he may be of service to you.

PHOEBE Governorship of Holloway Gaol?

GEOFFREY Not a bad guess. Very near it. To the Under-Secretaryship for Home Affairs.

LADY MOGTON Who is it?

GEOFFREY [He bows.] Your affectionate and devoted servant.

ANNYS You!

PHOEBE [Genuinely delighted. She is not a quick thinker.] Bravo! Congratulations, old boy! [She has risen—she slaps him on the back.]

ANNYS Geoffrey! [She puts her arms about him.] You never told me anything.

GEOFFREY I know, dear. I was afraid. It mightn't have come off. And then you would have been so disappointed.

ANNYS [There are tears in her eyes. She still clings to him.] I am so glad. Oh, I am so glad!

GEOFFREY It is all your doing. You have been such a splendid help. [He breaks gently away from her. Turns to ST. HERBERT, with a lighter tone.] Haven't you anything to say to a fellow? You're not usually dumb.

ST. HERBERT It has all been so sudden—as the early Victorian heroine was fond of remarking!

GEOFFREY [Laughs.] It has been sudden. We had, none of us, any idea till yesterday that old Bullock was thinking of resigning.

ELIZABETH [She has risen and moved towards the fire.] Won't it necessitate a bye-election?

[LADY MOGTON and ST. HERBERT have been thinking it out. On the others the word falls like a bombshell.]

GEOFFREY [He turns to her. He does not see their faces.] Yes. But I don't anticipate a contest. The Conservatives are without a candidate, and I am on good terms with the Labour Party. Perhaps Mr. Hunnable—

[He laughs, then, turning, catches sight of his wife's face. From ANNYS he looks to the others.]

LADY MOGTON [She has risen.] You haven't heard, then, of McCaw versus Potts?

GEOFFREY "McCaw versus Potts!" What the -

ST. HERBERT Was decided in the House of Lords late yesterday afternoon. Briefly stated, it confers upon women the right of becoming Parliamentary candidates.

GEOFFREY [He is staggered.] You mean -

LADY MOGTON Having regard to which, we have decided to bring forward a woman candidate to contest the next bye-election.

GEOFFREY Um! I see.

ANNYS But we never thought—we never anticipated it would be Geoffrey's.

LADY MOGTON I really cannot admit that that alters the case. Geoffrey himself would never dream, I am sure, of asking us to sacrifice our cause to his convenience.

GEOFFREY No. Of course not. Certainly not.

LADY MOGTON It is perhaps unfortunate that the candidate selected -

ANNYS It is quite impossible. Such a dilemma was never dreamed of.

LADY MOGTON And if not? Is the solidarity of woman -

GEOFFREY [Beginning to guess.] Forgive my impatience; but whom HAVE you selected?

ELIZABETH [When she likes she can be quite sweet.] Your wife. [He expected it.] We rather assumed [she appeals to the others with a gesture], I think, that the president of the Man's League for the Extension of the Franchise to Women would regard it as a compliment.

GEOFFREY [His dislike of her is already in existence.] Yes. Very thoughtful.

ANNYS You must choose some one else.

PHOEBE But there IS no one else.

ANNYS There's mamma.

PHOEBE Mamma's too heavy.

ANNYS Well, then, there's Elizabeth—there's you!

GEOFFREY Yes. Why not you? You and I could have a jolly little fight.

LADY MOGTON This is not a laughing matter. If I could think of any one to take Annys's place I should not insist. I cannot.

PHOEBE You see, it mustn't be a crank.

GEOFFREY [He is losing his temper.] Yes, I suppose that does limit you.

ELIZABETH And then—thanks to you—Mrs. Chilvers has had such excellent training in politics. It was that, I think, that decided us.

GEOFFREY [Convention forbids his strangling her.] Will somebody kindly introduce me to this lady?

ST. HERBERT Ah, yes, of course. You don't know each other, do you? Mr. Geoffrey Chilvers—Mrs. Joseph Spender. Mrs. Spender— Mr. Chilvers, M.P.

ELIZABETH [Sweetly.] Delighted!

GEOFFREY [Not.] Charmed.

LADY MOGTON [To ANNYS.] I am not indifferent to your difficulty. But the history of woman, my dear Annys, is a history of sacrifice. We give our sons—if necessary, our husbands.

MRS. MOUNTCALM-VILLIERS [Affected.] How true!

ANNYS But you are not asking me to give him. You are asking me to fight him. I can't.

LADY MOGTON You mean you won't.

ANNYS You can put it that way if you like. I won't.

[A pause.]

JANET I thought Mrs. Chilvers had pledged her word.

ELIZABETH Yes. But without her husband's consent. So, of course, it doesn't count.

GEOFFREY [He turns on her.] Why not you—if there must be a fight? Or would it be against your principles?

ELIZABETH Not in the least.

GEOFFREY Ah!

ELIZABETH I would offer myself as a substitute. Only it might seem like coming between husband and wife.

GEOFFREY [He turns away with a grunt of disgust.]

PHOEBE It's awfully rough on you, Geoffrey. I can see it from your point of view. But one can't help remembering the things that you yourself have said.

GEOFFREY I know; I know. I've been going up and down the country, excusing even your excesses on the ground that no movement can force its way to the front without treading on innumerable toes. For me, now, to cry halt merely because it happens to be my own toes that are in the way would be—ridiculous—absurd— would be monstrous. [Nobody contradicts him.] You are perfectly justified- -if this case means what you say it does—in putting up a candidate against me for East Poplar. Only, naturally, it cannot be Annys. [He reaches out his hand to where ANNYS stands a little behind him, takes her hand.] Annys and I have fought more than one election. It has been side by side.

ELIZABETH The lady a little behind.

GEOFFREY [He moves away with an expression of deep annoyance.]

JANET [She comes forward. She holds forth her hands with a half- appealing, half-commanding gesture. She almost seems inspired.] Would it not be so much better if, in this first political contest between man and woman, the opponents were two people honouring one another, loving one another? Would it not show to all the world that man and woman may meet—contend in public life without anger, without scorn? [There is a pause. They stand listening.] I do not know, but it seems to me that if Mr. Chilvers could bring himself to do this it would be such a big thing—perhaps the most chivalrous thing that a man has ever done to help women. If he would put aside, quite voluntarily, all the man's privilege—just say to the people, "Now choose—one of us two to serve you.

We stand before you, equal, my wife and I." I don't know how to put it, but I feel that by merely doing that one thing Mr. Chilvers would solve the whole problem. It would prove that good men are ready to give us of their free accord all that we claim. We should gain our rights, not by warfare, but through love and understanding. Wouldn't that be—so much better? [She looks—her hands still appealing—from one to the other.]

[Another silence. They have all been carried a little off their feet by JANET'S earnestness.]

ANNYS [She touches him.] What do you think, dear?

GEOFFREY Yes, there's a good deal, of course, in what Miss Blake says.

ANNYS It WOULD be a big thing for you to do.

PHOEBE You see, whatever happened, the seat would be yours. This case only gives us the right to go to the poll. We are keen upon Annys because she's our best card, that's all.

GEOFFREY Do you wish it?

ANNYS [She smiles up at him.] I'd rather fight you than any one else.

GEOFFREY You are not afraid that the situation might be—just a trifle comical?

ANNYS [Shakes her head.] No. I think everybody will say it was rather splendid of you.

GEOFFREY Well, if it will help women.

ANNYS [She holds out her hand. She is still in exalted mood.] We will show how man and woman may be drawn nearer to one another by rivalry for noble ends.

ST. HERBERT [He shakes GEOFFREY'S somewhat limp hand.] I envy you. The situation promises to be piquant.

MRS. MOUNTCALM-VILLIERS It will be a battle of roses.

LADY MOGTON I must go. I shall see you both again to-morrow. [She kisses GEOFFREY.] This is an historic day.

GEOFFREY Yes. I daresay we shall all remember it.

LADY MOGTON [To JANET.] I will get you to come to the station with me. I can give you your instructions in the cab. [She kisses ANNYS.] You have been called to a great work. Be worthy of it.

[They are all making ready to go. ANNYS has rung the bell for HAKE.]

JANET [To ANNYS.] Are you glad?

ANNYS [Kisses her.] You showed me the whole thing in a new light. You were splendid. [She turns to ELIZABETH.] Didn't I tell you he would convert you?

ELIZABETH I was wrong to judge all men guilty. There are also— the innocent.

ANNYS [For a moment—but a moment only—she is pleased. Then the doubtful meaning of ELIZABETH'S words strikes her.]

[Enter HAKE.]

ANNYS [She has to dismiss ELIZABETH.] Oh, Hake— [To LADY MOGTON.] You'll want a cab, won't you, mamma?

LADY MOGTON A taxi— Goodbye, everybody.

[She sails out.]

MRS. MOUNTCALM-VILLIERS I have my carriage. [To ELIZABETH.] Can I give you a lift?

ELIZABETH Thank you. [To GEOFFREY.] We shall meet again.

GEOFFREY I feel sure of it.

[MRS. MOUNTCALM-VILLIERS and ELIZABETH go out.]

PHOEBE [To HAKE.] Are Miss Blake's things dry yet?

JANET They'll be quite all right, dear. Please don't trouble. [She advances a timid hand to GEOFFREY.] Goodbye, Mr. Chilvers.

GEOFFREY [He takes it smiling.] Goodbye.

[She goes out; HAKE follows.]

PHOEBE Goodbye, old boy. [They shake hands.] Don't you let her walk over you. Make her fight.

ANNYS [Laughing.] Don't you worry about that.

ST. HERBERT Would you care to look through McCaw v. Potts? [He has the papers in his hand.]

GEOFFREY I'll ask you for it when I want it.

PHOEBE [At door.] You'll be alone this evening?

ANNYS Yes. Come in to dinner.

PHOEBE All right. Goodbye.

ST. HERBERT Goodbye.

[GEOFFREY and ANNYS answer them. They go out, closing the door. GEOFFREY is by the fire. ANNYS comes to him.]

ANNYS [She puts her arms round him.] You don't mind?

GEOFFREY [He holds her at arms' length—looking into her eyes and smiling.] I believe you are looking forward to it.

ANNYS Do you know how long we have been married? Eight years. And do you know, sir, that all that time we have never had a difference? Don't you think it will be good for you?

GEOFFREY Do you know WHY we have never had a difference? Because you have always had your own way.

ANNYS Oh!

GEOFFREY You have got so used to it, you don't notice it.

ANNYS Then it will be good for me. I must learn to suffer opposition. [She laughs.]

GEOFFREY You won't like it.

ANNYS Do you know, I'm not at all sure that I shan't. [Unconsciously they let loose of one another.] You see, I shall have the right of hitting back. [Again she laughs.]

GEOFFREY [Also laughingly.] Is woman going to develop the fighting instinct?

ANNYS I wonder.

[A moment's silence.]

GEOFFREY The difficulty in our case is there seems nothing to fight about.

ANNYS We must think of something. [Laughs.]

GEOFFREY What line are you going to take—what is your argument: why they should vote for you in preference to me?

ANNYS Simply that I am a woman.

GEOFFREY My dear child, that won't be enough. Why should they vote for you merely because you're a woman?

ANNYS [Slightly astonished.] Because—because women are wanted in public life.

GEOFFREY Who wants them?

ANNYS [More astonished.] Who? Why—[it doesn't seem too clear.] Why, all of us—you, yourself!

GEOFFREY I'm not East Poplar.

ANNYS [Is puzzled a moment, then valiantly.] I shall ask them to send me to Parliament to represent the interests of their women— and therefore of themselves—the interests of their children.

GEOFFREY Children! What do you know about children?

[Another silence.]

ANNYS Personally—no. We have had no children of our own, of course. But [hopefully] it is a woman's instinct.

GEOFFREY Oh, Lord! That's what the lady said who had buried seven.

ANNYS [Her mouth is growing hard.] Don't you believe in the right of women to share in the government of the country?

GEOFFREY Some women. Yes. I can see some capable -

ANNYS [Winces.]

GEOFFREY —elderly, motherly woman who has brought up a dozen children of her own—who knows the world, being of some real use.

ANNYS If it comes to that, there must be—I don't say more "capable," but more experienced, more fatherly men than yourself.

[He turns, they look at one another. His tone almost touched contempt—hers was veiled anger.]

GEOFFREY THAT'S the danger. It may come to a real fight.

ANNYS [Upon her also the fear has fallen.] It must not. [She flings her arms around him.] We must show the world that man and woman can meet—contend in public life without anger, without scorn.

GEOFFREY [He folds her to him.] The very words sound ugly, don't they?

ANNYS It would be hideous. [She draws away.] How long will the election last?

GEOFFREY Not long. The writ will be issued on Wednesday. Nomination on Monday—polling, I expect, on Saturday. Puts me in mind—I must prepare my election address.

ANNYS I ought to be getting on with mine, too, I suppose.

GEOFFREY It ought to be out by to-morrow.

ANNYS [With inspiration.] We'll do yours first. [She wonders why he hesitates.]

GEOFFREY "We?" Shan't I have to do it alone—this time?

ANNYS Alone! Nonsense! How can you?

GEOFFREY I'm afraid I shall have to try.

ANNYS Um! I suppose you're right. What a nuisance! [She turns away.] I shan't like it.

GEOFFREY [He moves towards the folding-doors.] No. It won't be quite the same thing. Goodbye.

ANNYS [She crosses to her desk by the window. Not the same instant but the next his "Goodbye" strikes her. She turns.] You're not going out, are you?

GEOFFREY [He stops and turns—puzzled at her question.] No. Only into my study.

ANNYS You said "Goodbye."

GEOFFREY [Not remembering.] *I* did! Must have been thinking of something else. I shall be in here if you want me. [He goes into the other room.]

ANNYS [She has crossed to her desk. She is humming. She seats herself, takes paper and pen, writes. Without turning—still writing—she raises her voice.] Geoffrey! How do you spell "experimental"? One "r" or two?

[There is no answer. Puzzled at the silence, she looks round. The great folding-doors are closed. She stares in front of her, thinking, then turns again to her work.]

CURTAIN.

THE SECOND ACT

SCENE:- Liberal Central Committee Rooms, East India Dock Road, Poplar. A large, high room on the first floor of an old-fashioned house. Two high windows right. A door at back is the main entrance. A door left leads to other rooms. The walls are papered with election literature. Conspicuous among the posters displayed is "A Man for Men." "No Petticoat Government." "Will you be Henpecked?" A large, round table centre is littered with papers and pamphlets. A large desk stands between the windows. A settee is against the left wall.

[When the curtain rises, ROSE MERTON (otherwise "GINGER") is discovered seated, her left arm resting on the table. She is a young lady typical of the Cockney slavey type, dressed according to the ideas of her class as regards the perfect lady. Her hat is characteristic. Her gloves, her reticule, her umbrella—the latter something rather "saucy"—are displayed around her. She is feeling comfortable and airing her views. MRS. CHINN is laying the cloth over a portion of the table, with some tea-things. MRS. CHINN is a thin, narrow-chested lady with thin hands and bony wrists. No one since her husband died has ever seen her without her bonnet. Its appearance suggests the possibility that she sleeps in it. It is black, like her dress. The whole figure is decent, but dingy.]

GINGER Wot I say about the question is -

MRS. CHINN Do you mind moving your arm?

GINGER Beg pardon. [She shifts.] Wot I say is, why not give us the vote and end all the talking?

MRS. CHINN You think it would have that effect?

GINGER Well! we don't want to go on being a nuisance—longer than we can possibly 'elp!

MRS. CHINN Daresay you're right. It's about the time most people stop.

GINGER You've never thought much about the question yourself, 'ave you, Mrs. Chinn?

MRS. CHINN I ain't fretted much about it.

GINGER Was a time when I didn't. I used to be all for—you know— larking about. I never thought much about anything.

MRS. CHINN Ah! it's a useful habit.

GINGER What is?

MRS. CHINN Thinking.

GINGER It's what we women 'aven't done enough of— in the past, I mean. All that's going to be altered. In the future there's going to be no difference between men and women.

MRS. CHINN [Slowly, quietly she turns upon GINGER her expressionless eyes.]

GINGER Mentally, I mean, o' course.

MRS. CHINN [Takes back her eyes.]

GINGER Do you know, Mrs. Chinn, that once upon a time there was only one sex? [She spreads herself.] Hus!

MRS. CHINN You ain't thinking of going back to it, are you?

GINGER Not if the men be'ave themselves.

MRS. CHINN Perhaps they're doing their best, poor things! It don't do to be too impatient with them.

GINGER Was talking to old Dot-and-carry-one the other d'y. You know who I mean—chap with the wooden leg as 'as 'is pitch outside the "George." "Wot do you wimmen want worrying yourselves about things outside the 'ome?" 'e says to me. "You've got the children," 'e says. "Oh," I says, "and whose fault's that, I'd like to know? You wait till we've got the vote," I says, "we'll soon show you—"

[SIGSBY enters. SIGSBY is a dapper little man, very brisk and bustling—hirsute—looks as if he wanted dusting, cleaning up generally.]

SIGSBY That young blackguard come back yet?

GINGER [At sound of SIGSBY'S voice she springs up. At first is about to offer excuses for being found seated, but recollects herself.]

MRS. CHINN Which one, sir?

SIGSBY Young Jawbones—what's he call himself?—Gordon.

MRS. CHINN Not yet, sir.

SIGSBY [Grunts.] My chop ready?

MRS. CHINN I expect it's about done. I'll see.

[She goes out.]

SIGSBY [He turns to GINGER.] What can *I* do for you?

GINGER [She produces a letter.] I was to wait for an answer.

SIGSBY [He opens and reads it.] What do they expect me to do?

GINGER 'Er ladyship thought as perhaps you would consult Mr. Chilvers 'imself on the subject.

SIGSBY Look here. What I want to know is this: am I being asked to regard Lady Mogton as my opponent's election agent, or as my principal's mother-in-law? That point's got to be settled. [His vehemence deepens.] Look at all these posters. Not to be used, for fear the other side mayn't like them. Now Lady Mogton writes me that my candidate's supporters are not to employ a certain argument she disapproves of: because, if they do, she'll tell his wife. Is this an election, or is it a family jar?

[JAWBONES enters. JAWBONES—otherwise WILLIAM GORDON—is a clean- shaven young hooligan. He wears a bicycle cap on the back of his head, allowing a picturesque tuft of hair to fall over his forehead. Evidently he is suffering from controlled indignation.]

SIGSBY [Seeing him.] Oh, so you've come back, have you?

JAWBONES I 'ave, wot's left of me.

SIGSBY What have you been doing?

JAWBONES Clinging to a roof for the last three hours.

SIGSBY Clinging to a roof! What for?

JAWBONES [He boils over.] Wot for? 'Cos I didn't want to fall off! Wot do you think: 'cos I was fond of it?

SIGSBY I don't understand -

JAWBONES You find yourself 'alf way up a ladder, posting bills as the other side 'as took objection to—with a crowd of girls from Pink's jam factory waiting for you at the bottom with a barrel of treacle, and you WILL understand. Nothing else for me to do, o' course, but to go up. Then they took the ladder away.

SIGSBY Where are the bills?

JAWBONES Last I see of them was their being put into a 'earse on its way to Ilford Cemetery.

SIGSBY This has got to be seen into. This sort of thing can't be allowed to go on. [He snatches up his hat.]

JAWBONES There's another suggestion I'd like to make.

SIGSBY [Pauses.]

JAWBONES That is, if this election is going to be fought fairly, that our side should be provided with 'at-pins.

SIGSBY [Grunts.] Tell Mrs. Chinn to keep that chop warm. [He goes out.]

GINGER [She begins to giggle. It grows into a shrill hee-haw.]

JAWBONES [He looks at her fixedly.]

GINGER [Her laugh, under the stern eye of JAWBONES, dies away.]

JAWBONES Ain't no crowd of you 'ere, you know. Nothing but my inborn chivalry to prevent my pulling your nose.

GINGER [Cowed, but simmering.] Chivalry! [A shrill snort.]

JAWBONES Yus. And don't you put a strain upon it neither.
Because I tell you straight, it's weakening.

GINGER [His sudden fierceness has completely cowed her.]

JAWBONES You wimmin -

[There re-enters Mrs. CHINN with a tray. He is between them.]

That's old Sigsby's chop?

MRS. CHINN Yes. He hasn't gone out again, has he?

JAWBONES I'll 'ave it. Get 'im another. Guess 'e won't be back for 'alf an hour.

MRS. CHINN He's nasty when his food ain't ready.

JAWBONES [He takes the tray from her.] Not your fault. Tell 'im I took it from you by brute force.

MRS. CHINN [She acquiesces with her usual even absence of all emotion.]

JAWBONES You needn't stop. Miss Rose Merton will do the waiting.

GINGER [Starts, then begins to collect her etceteras.]

MRS. CHINN Perhaps there'll be time to cook him another.

[She goes out.]

JAWBONES Take off that cover.

GINGER [She starts on a bolt for the door.]

JAWBONES [He is quite prepared. In an instant he is in front of her.] No, yer don't.

[A pause.]

Take off that cover.

GINGER [She still hesitates.]

JAWBONES If yer don't do what I tell yer, I'll 'ide yer. I'm in the mood.

GINGER [She takes off the cover.]

JAWBONES [He seats himself and falls to.] Now pour me out a cup of tea.

GINGER [Is pouring it out.]

JAWBONES Know why yer doing it?

GINGER [With shrill indignation.] Yus. Becos yer got me 'ere alone, yer beast, with only that cracked image of a Mrs. Chinn -

JAWBONES That'll do.

GINGER [It is sufficient. She stops.]

JAWBONES None of your insults agen a lady as I 'olds in 'igh respect. The rest of it is all right. Becos I've got yer 'ere alone. You wimmin, you think it's going to pay you to chuck law and order. You're out for a fight, are yer?

GINGER Yus, and we're going to win. Brute force 'as 'ad its d'y. It's brains wot are going to rule the world. And we've got 'em.

[She has become quite oratorical.]

JAWBONES Glad to 'ear it. Take my tip: you'll use 'em. Meanwhile I'll 'ave another cup o' tea.

GINGER [She takes the cup—is making for the window.]

JAWBONES [Fierce again.] I said tea.

GINGER All right, I was only going to throw the slops out of window. There ain't no basin.

JAWBONES I'll tell yer when I want yer to open the window and call for the p'lice. You can throw them into the waste-paper basket.

GINGER [She obeys.]

JAWBONES Thank you. Very much obliged. One of these d'ys, maybe, you'll marry.

GINGER When I do, it will be a man, not a monkey.

JAWBONES I'm not proposing. I'm talking to you for your good.

GINGER [Snorts.]

JAWBONES You've been listening to a lot of toffs. Easy enough for them to talk about wimmen not being domestic drudges. They keep a cook to do it. They don't pity 'e for being a down-trodden slive, spending sixteen hours a d'y in THEIR kitchen with an evening out once a week. When you marry it will be to a bloke like me, a working man . . .

GINGER Working! [She follows it with a shrill laugh.]

JAWBONES Yus. There's always a class as laughs when you mention the word "work." Them as knows wot it is, don't. I've been at it since six o'clock this morning, carrying a ladder, a can of paste weighing twenty pounds, and two 'undred double royal posters. You try it! When 'e comes 'ome, 'e'll want 'is victuals. If you've got 'em ready for 'im and are looking nice—no reason why you shouldn't—and feeling amiable, you'll get on very well together. If you are going to argue with 'im about woman's sphere, you'll get the worst of it.

GINGER You always was a bully.

JAWBONES Not always. Remember last Bank 'oliday? [He winks.]

GINGER [She tries not to give in.]

JAWBONES 'Ave a cup of tea. [He pours it out for her.]

GINGER [The natural woman steals in—she sits.]

JAWBONES 'Ow are they doing you, fairly well?

GINGER Oh! Well, nothing to grumble at.

JAWBONES You can do a bit o' dressing on it.

GINGER [She meets his admiring eye. The suffragette departs.]
Dressing don't cost much—when you've got tyste.

JAWBONES Wot! Not that 'at?

GINGER Made it myself.

JAWBONES No!

GINGER Honour bright! Tell yer -

[GEOFFREY and ST. HERBERT enter. JAWBONES and GINGER make to rise. GINGER succeeds.]

GEOFFREY All right, all right. Don't let me disturb the party. Where's Mr. Sigsby?

JAWBONES Gone to look up the police, I think, sir. [Having finished, he rises.] Some of those factory girls been up to their larks again.

GEOFFREY Umph! What's it about this time?

JAWBONES They've took objection to one of our posters.

GEOFFREY What, another! [To ST. HERBERT.] Woman has disappointed me as a fighter. She's willing enough to strike. If you hit back, she's surprised and grieved.

ST. HERBERT She's come to the game rather late.

GEOFFREY She might have learned the rules. [To JAWBONES.] Which particular one is it that has failed to meet with their approval?

JAWBONES It's rather a good one, sir, from our point of view: "Why she left her 'appy 'ome."

GEOFFREY I don't seem to remember it. Have I seen it?

JAWBONES I don't think you 'ave, sir. It was Mr. Sigsby's idea. On the left, the ruined 'ome, baby crying it's little 'eart out— eldest child lying on the floor, scalded—upset the tea-kettle over itself—youngest boy in flames—been playing with the matches, nobody there to stop 'im. At the open door the father, returning from work. Nothing ready for 'im. On the other side—'ER, on a tub, spouting politics.

GEOFFREY [To ST. HERBERT.] Sounds rather good.

JAWBONES Wait a minute. There was a copy somewhere about—a proof. [He is searching for it on the desk—finds it.] Yus, 'ere 'tis. [To GINGER.] Catch 'old.

[JAWBONES and GINGER hold it displayed.] That's the one, sir.

ST. HERBERT Why is the working man, for pictorial purposes, always a carpenter?

GINGER It's the skirt we object to.

GEOFFREY The skirt! What's wrong with the skirt?

GINGER Well, it's only been out of fashion for the last three years, that's all.

GEOFFREY Oh! I see. [To ST. HERBERT.] We've been hitting them below the belt. What do you think I ought to do about it?

ST. HERBERT What would you have thought yourself, three weeks ago?

GEOFFREY You and I have been friends ever since we were boys. You rather like me, don't you?

ST. HERBERT [Puzzled.] Yes.

GEOFFREY If I were to suddenly hit you on the nose, what would happen?

ST. HERBERT I understand. Woman has suddenly started hitting man on the nose. Her excuse being that she really couldn't keep her hands off him any longer.

JAWBONES [He has pinned the poster to the wall.] They begun it. To 'ear them talk, you'd think as man had never done anything right.

GEOFFREY He's quite right. Their posters are on every hoarding: "Who's made all the Muddles? Man!" "Men's Promises! Why, it's all Froth!" "Woman this Time!" I suppose it will have to go.

JAWBONES [Hopefully.] Up, sir?

GEOFFREY No, Jawbones. Into the dust-heap with the rest.

[JAWBONES is disgusted. GINGER is triumphant.]

GEOFFREY I must talk to Sigsby. He's taking the whole thing too seriously. It will be some time before we reach that stage. [To JAWBONES.] Ask Mrs. Chinn to bring me a cup of tea.

[JAWBONES goes out.]

[He seats himself at table and takes up some correspondence. To GINGER.] Are you waiting for any one?

GINGER A letter from her ladyship. [She picks up from the desk and hands him the letter SIGSBY had thrown there.] Her ladyship thought you ought to be consulted.

GEOFFREY [He reads the short letter with a gathering frown—hands it across to ST. HERBERT.]

ST. HERBERT [Having read, he passes it back in silence.]

GEOFFREY [To GINGER.] Do you know the contents of this letter?

GINGER The matter has been discussed among us—informally.

GEOFFREY Tell Lady Mogton I'll—talk to her myself on the subject.

GINGER Thank you. [She collects her etceteras.] Good afternoon.

GEOFFREY [Shortly.] Good afternoon.

GINGER [She bows graciously to ST. HERBERT, who responds. Goes out.]

GEOFFREY The devil of it is that it's the truth.

ST. HERBERT Somebody was bound to say it, sooner or later!

GEOFFREY Yes, but one's own wife! This is a confoundedly awkward situation.

ST. HERBERT [He comes to him, stands looking down at him.] Did it never occur to you, when you were advocating equal political rights for women, that awkward situations might arise?

GEOFFREY [He leans back in his chair.] Do you remember Tommy the Terrier, as they used to call him in the House—was always preaching Socialism?

ST. HERBERT Quite the most amusing man I ever met!

GEOFFREY And not afraid of being honest. Do you remember his answer when somebody asked him what he would do if Socialism, by any chance, really became established in England? He had just married an American heiress. He said he should emigrate. I am still convinced that woman is entitled to equal political rights with man. I didn't think it was coming in my time. There are points in the problem remaining to be settled before we can arrive at a working solution. This is one of them. [He takes up the letter and reads.] "Are you prepared to have as your representative a person who for six months out of every year may be incapacitated from serving you?" It's easy enough to say I oughtn't to allow my supporters to drag in the personal element. I like it even less myself. But what's the answer?

[JAWBONES enters with a tray.]

JAWBONES [Places tray on table.] Tea's coming in a minute, sir. [He is clearing away.]

GEOFFREY Never mind all that. [He hands him a slip.] Take this to the printers. Tell them I must have a proof to-night.

JAWBONES Yes, sir. [Finds his cap and goes out.]

ST. HERBERT The answer, I should say, would be that the majority of women will continue to find something better to do. The women who will throw themselves into politics will be the unattached women, the childless women. [In an instant he sees his mistake, but it is too late.]

GEOFFREY [He rises, crosses to the desk, throws into a waste- paper-basket a piece of crumpled paper that was in his hand; then turns. The personal note has entered into the discussion.] The women who WANT to be childless—what about them?

ST. HERBERT [He shrugs his shoulders.] Are there any such?

GEOFFREY There are women who talk openly of woman's share in the general scheme being a "burden" on her—an "incubus."

ST. HERBERT A handful of cranks. To the normal woman motherhood has always been the one supreme desire.

GEOFFREY Because children crowned her with honour. The barren woman was despised. All that is changing. This movement is adding impulse to it.

ST. HERBERT Movements do not alter instincts.

GEOFFREY But they do. Ever since man emerged from the jungle he has been shedding his instincts—shaping them to new desires. Where do you find this all-prevailing instinct towards maternity? Among the women of society, who sacrifice it without a moment's hesitation to their vanity—to their mere pleasures? The middle- class woman—she, too, is demanding "freedom." Children, servants, the home!—they are too much for her "nerves." And now there comes this new development, appealing to the intellectual woman. Is there not danger of her preferring political ambition, the excitement of public life, to what has come to be regarded as the "drudgery" of turning four walls into a home, of peopling the silence with the voices of the children? [He crosses to the table- -lays his hand again upon the open letter.] How do you know that this may not be her answer—"I have no children. I never mean to have children"?

[SIGSBY enters in company with BEN LAMB, M.P. LAMB is a short, thick-set, good-tempered man.]

Ah, Lamb, how are you?

LAMB [They greet one another.] How are things going?

SIGSBY They're not going at all well.

GEOFFREY Sigsby was ever the child of despondency.

SIGSBY Yes, and so will you be when you find yourself at the bottom of the poll.

GEOFFREY [The notion takes him by surprise.]

LAMB It's going to be a closer affair than any of us thought.
It's the joke of the thing that appears to have got hold of them.
They want to see what will happen.

GEOFFREY Man's fatal curiosity concerning the eternal feminine!

SIGSBY Yes, and they won't have to pay for it. That will be our department.

ST. HERBERT [To SIGSBY.] What do you think they'll do, supposing by any chance Mrs. Chilvers should head the poll?

SIGSBY How do you mean—"what'll they do?"

ST. HERBERT Do you think they'll claim the seat?

SIGSBY Claim the seat! What do you think they're out for—their health? Get another six months' advertisement, if they don't get anything else. Meanwhile what's our position—just at the beginning of our ministerial career?

GEOFFREY They will not claim the seat.

SIGSBY How do you know?

GEOFFREY I know my wife.

LAMB [After a moment's silence.] Quite sure you do?

GEOFFREY [Turns.]

LAMB Ever seen a sheep fighting mad? I have. Damned sight worse than the old ram.

GEOFFREY She doesn't fight the ram.

LAMB [He makes a sweeping movement that takes in the room, the election—all things.] What's all this? We thought woman hadn't got the fighting instinct—that we "knew her." My boy, we're in the infants' class.

SIGSBY If you want to be his Majesty's Under-Secretary for Home Affairs, you take my tip, guv'nor, you'll win this election.

GEOFFREY What more can I do than I'm doing? How can I countenance this sort of thing? [He indicates the posters.] Declare myself dead against the whole movement?

LAMB You'll do it later. May as well do it soon.

GEOFFREY Why must I do it?

LAMB Because you're beginning to find out what it means.

[A pause. The door is open. ANNYS is standing there.]

ANNYS Dare we venture into the enemy's camp?

[She enters, laughing, followed by ELIZABETH and PHOEBE. ANNYS is somewhat changed from the grave, dreamy ANNYS of a short week ago. She is brimming over with vitality—excitement. There is a decisiveness, an egoism, about her that seems new to her. The women's skirts make a flutter. A breeze seems to have entered. ANNYS runs to her husband. For the moment the election fades away. They are all smiles, tenderness for one another.]

ANNYS Don't tell, will you? Mamma would be so shocked. Do you know you haven't been near me for three days?

GEOFFREY Umph! I like that. Where were you last night?

ANNYS Last night? In the neighbourhood of Leicester Square till three o'clock. Oh, Geoff, there's such a lot wants altering!

[She turns to greet the others.]

GEOFFREY Your ruining your health won't do it. You're looking fagged to death.

ANNYS [She shakes hands with SIGSBY.] How are you? [To LAMB.] I'm so glad you're helping him. [She turns again to GEOFFREY.] Pure imagination, dearest. I never felt better in my life.

GEOFFREY Umph! Look at all those lines underneath your eyes. [He shakes hands with ELIZABETH.] How do you do? [To PHOEBE.] How are you?

ANNYS [She comes back to him—makes to smooth the lines from his forehead.] Look at all those, there. We'll run away together for a holiday, when it's all over. What are you doing this evening?

SIGSBY You promised to speak at a Smoker to-night; the Bow and Bromley Buffaloes.

ANNYS Oh, bother the Buffaloes. Take me out to dinner. I am free after seven.

[MRS. CHINN has entered—is arranging the table for tea. ANNYS goes to her.]

How are you, Mrs. Chinn?

MRS. CHINN [She wipes her hand on her apron before taking ANNYS'S proffered hand.]

GEOFFREY [To SIGSBY.] I can turn up there later in the evening. [He joins the others for a moment—talks with them.]

MRS. CHINN [Now shaking hands.] Quite well, thank you, ma'am. [She has cast a keen, motherly glance at ANNYS.] I hope you're taking care of yourself, ma'am.

ANNYS Of course I am. We Politicians owe it to our Party. [Laughs.] How are they getting on here, without me?

MRS. CHINN Well, ma'am, from what I can see, I think Mr. Chilvers is trusting a little too much to his merits. Shall I bring some more cups and saucers, sir?

GEOFFREY Ah! yes! [To ANNYS.] You'll have some tea?

ANNYS Strong, please, Mrs. Chinn.

[MRS. CHINN goes out.]

[Laughs.] Yes, I know it's bad for me. [She puts a hand over his mouth.]

PHOEBE Old Mother Chinn is quite right, you know, Geoff. You're not putting up a good fight.

GEOFFREY [A slight irritability begins to show itself.] I frankly confess that I am not used to fighting women.

ELIZABETH Yes. It was easier, no doubt, when we took it lying down.

ANNYS You promised, if I brought you, that you would be good.

GEOFFREY I wish it had been you.

PHOEBE Yes, but we don't!

[As she and ELIZABETH move away.]

Did you have a row with the doctor when you were born?

[To which ELIZABETH replies, though the words reach only PHOEBE: "I might have, if I had known that my mother was doing all the work, while he was pocketing the fee!"]

LAMB You see, Mrs. Chilvers, our difficulty is that there is nothing to be said against you—except one thing.

ANNYS What's that?

LAMB That you're a woman.

ANNYS [Smiling.] Isn't that enough?

SIGSBY Quite enough, Mrs. Chilvers, if the guv'nor would only say it.

ANNYS [To GEOFFREY.] Why don't you? I'll promise not to deny it.

[The others drift apart. They group themselves near to the window. They talk together—grow evidently interested and excited.]

GEOFFREY I have just had a letter from your—Election Agent, expressing indignation with one of my supporters for merely having hinted at the fact.

ANNYS I don't understand.

GEOFFREY [He takes from the table the letter and hands it to her in silence. He seats himself on the settee and watches her.]

ANNYS [She seats herself on a chair just opposite to him; reads the letter through in silence.] In my case it does not apply.

GEOFFREY How do you know?

ANNYS [The atmosphere has grown suddenly oppressive.] Oh, I—I think we might find some other reason than that. [She hands him back the letter.]

GEOFFREY It's the only one of any importance. It embraces all the others. Shall woman be mother—or politician? [He puts the letter in his pocket.]

ANNYS Why cannot she be both?

GEOFFREY [He is looking at her searchingly.] Because if she is the one, she doesn't want to be the other.

[A silence.]

ANNYS You are wrong. It is the mother instinct that makes us politicians. We want to take care of the world.

GEOFFREY Exactly. You think man's job more interesting than your own.

ANNYS [After a moment.] Who told you that it was a man's job?

GEOFFREY Well. [He shrugs his shoulders.] We can't do yours.

ANNYS Can't we help each other?

GEOFFREY As, for instance, in this election! [He gives a short laugh.]

ANNYS Of course, this is an exceptional case.

GEOFFREY It's an epitome of the whole question. You are trying to take my job away from me. To the neglect of your own.

ANNYS [After another moment's silence.] Haven't I always tried to do my duty?

GEOFFREY I have thought so.

ANNYS Oh, my dear, we mustn't quarrel. You will win this election. I want you to win it. Next time we must fight side by side again.

GEOFFREY Don't you see? Fighting you means fighting the whole movement. [He indicates the posters pinned to the walls.] That sort of thing.

ANNYS [After a brief inspection.] Not that way. [Shaking her head.] It would break my heart for you to turn against us. Win because you are the better man. [Smiling.] I want you to be the better man.

GEOFFREY I would rather be your husband.

ANNYS [Smiling.] Isn't that the same thing?

GEOFFREY No. I want a wife.

ANNYS What precisely do you mean by "wife"?

GEOFFREY It's an old-established word.

[MRS. CHINN has entered to complete the tea arrangements. She is arranging the table.]

MRS. CHINN There's a deputation downstairs, sir, just come for you.

GEOFFREY What are they?

MRS. CHINN It's one of those societies for the reform of something. They said you were expecting them.

SIGSBY [Breaking away from the group by the window.] Quite right. [Looks at his watch.] Five o'clock, I'll bring them up.

GEOFFREY Happen to know what it is they want to reform?

SIGSBY [By door.] Laws relating to the physical relationship between the sexes, I think.

GEOFFREY Oh, only that!

SIGSBY Something of the sort.

[He goes out. MRS. CHINN also by the other door.]

GEOFFREY [Rising.] Will you pour out?

ANNYS [She has been thinking. She comes back to the present.] We shan't be in your way?

GEOFFREY Oh, no. It will make it easier to get rid of them.

[ANNYS changes her chair. The others gather round. The service and drinking of tea proceeds in the usual course.]

[To ELIZABETH.] You'll take some tea?

ELIZABETH Thank you.

GEOFFREY You must be enjoying yourself just now.

ELIZABETH [Makes a moue.] They insist on my being agreeable.

ANNYS It's so good for her. Teaches her self-control.

LAMB I gather from Mrs. Spender, that in the perfect world there will be no men at all.

ELIZABETH Oh, yes, they will be there. But in their proper place.

ST. HERBERT That's why you didn't notice them.

[The DEPUTATION reaches the door. The sound of voices is heard.]

PHOEBE She's getting on very well. If she isn't careful, she'll end up by being a flirt.

[The DEPUTATION enters, guided by SIGSBY. Its number is five, two men and three women. Eventually they group themselves—some standing, some sitting—each side of GEOFFREY. The others gather round ANNYS, who keeps her seat at the opposite side of the table.]

SIGSBY [Talking as he enters.] Exactly what I've always maintained.

HOPPER It would make the husband quite an interesting person.

SIGSBY [Cheerfully.] That's the idea. Here we are, guv'nor. This is Mr. Chilvers.

[GEOFFREY bows, the DEPUTATION also. SIGSBY introduces a remarkably boyish-looking man, dressed in knickerbockers.]

SIGSBY This is Mr. Peekin, who has kindly consented to act as spokesman. [To the DEPUTATION, generally.] Will you have some tea?

MISS BORLASSE [A thick-set, masculine-featured lady, with short hair and heavy eyebrows. Her deep, decisive tone settles the question.] Thank you. We have so little time.

MR. PEEKIN We propose, Mr. Chilvers, to come to the point at once. [He is all smiles, caressing gestures.]

GEOFFREY Excellent.

PEEKIN If I left a baby at your door, what would you do with it?

GEOFFREY [For a moment he is taken aback, recovers himself.] Are you thinking of doing so?

PEEKIN It's not impossible.

GEOFFREY Well, it sounds perhaps inhospitable, but do you know I really think I should ask you to take it away again.

PEEKIN Yes, but by the time you find it there, I shall have disappeared—skedaddled.

HOPPER Good. [He rubs his hands. Smiles at the others.]

GEOFFREY In that case I warn you that I shall hand it over to the police.

PEEKIN [He turns to the others.] I don't myself see what else Mr. Chilvers could be expected to do.

MISS BORLASSE He'd be a fool not to.

GEOFFREY Thank you. So far we seem to be in agreement. And now may I ask to what all this is leading?

PEEKIN [He changes from the debonnair to the dramatic.] How many men, Mr. Chilvers, leave their babies every year at the door of poverty-stricken women? What are they expected to do with them?

[A moment. The DEPUTATION murmur approval.]

GEOFFREY I see. But is there no difference between the two doors? I am not an accomplice.

PEEKIN An accomplice! Is the ignorant servant-girl—first lured into the public-house, cajoled, tricked, deceived by false promises—the half-starved shop-girl in the hands of the practised libertine—is she an accomplice?

MRS. PEEKIN [A dowdily-dressed, untidy woman, but the face is sweet and tender.] Ah, Mr. Chilvers, if you could only hear the stories that I have heard from dying lips.

GEOFFREY Very pitiful, my dear lady. And, alas, only too old. But there are others. It would not be fair to blame always the man.

ANNYS [Unnoticed, drawn by the subject, she has risen and come down.] Perhaps not. But the punishment always falls on the woman. Is THAT quite fair?

GEOFFREY [He is irritated at ANNYS'S incursion into the discussion.] My dear Annys, that is Nature's law, not man's. All man can do is to mitigate it.

PEEKIN That is all we ask. The suffering, the shame, must always be the woman's. Surely that is sufficient.

GEOFFREY What do you propose?

MISS BORLASSE [In her deep, fierce tones.] That all children born out of wedlock should be a charge upon the rates.

MISS RICKETTS [A slight, fair, middle-aged woman, with a nervous hesitating manner.] Of course, only if the mother wishes it.

GEOFFREY [The proposal staggers him. But the next moment it inspires him with mingled anger and amusement.] My dear, good people, have you stopped for one moment to consider what the result of your proposal would be?

PEEKIN For one thing, Mr. Chilvers, the adding to the populace of healthy children in place of the stunted and diseased abortions that is all that these poor women, out of their scanty earnings, can afford to present to the State.

GEOFFREY Humph! That incidentally it would undermine the whole institution of marriage, let loose the flood-gates that at present hold immorality in check, doesn't appear to trouble you. That the law must be altered to press less heavily upon the woman—that the man must be made an equal sharer in the penalty—all that goes without saying. The remedy you propose would be a thousand times worse than the disease.

ANNYS And meanwhile? Until you have devised this scheme [there is a note of contempt in her voice] under which escape for the man will be impossible?

GEOFFREY The evil must continue. As other evils have to until the true remedy is found.

PEEKIN [He has hurriedly consulted with the others. All have risen—he turns to GEOFFREY.] You will not support our demand?

GEOFFREY Support it! Do you mean that you cannot yourselves see that you are holding out an indemnity to every profligate, male and female, throughout the land— that you would be handicapping, in the struggle for existence, every honest man and woman desirous of bringing up their children in honour and in love? Your suggestion is monstrous!

PEEKIN [The little man is not without his dignity.] We apologise, Mr. Chilvers, for having taken up your time.

GEOFFREY I am sorry the matter was one offering so little chance of agreement.

PEEKIN We will make only one slight further trespass on your kindness. Mrs. Chilvers, if one may judge, would seem to be more in sympathy with our views. Might we—it would be a saving of time and shoe leather [he smiles]—might we take this opportunity of laying our case before her?

GEOFFREY It would be useless.

[A short silence. ANNYS, with ELIZABETH and PHOEBE a little behind her, stands right. LAMB, SIGSBY, and ST. HERBERT are behind GEOFFREY centre. The DEPUTATION is left.]

HOPPER Do we gather that in this election you speak for both candidates?

GEOFFREY In matters of common decency, yes. My wife does not associate herself with movements for the encouragement of vice.

[There is another moment's silence.]

ANNYS But, Geoffrey, dear—we should not be encouraging the evil. We should still seek to find the man, to punish him. The woman would still suffer -

GEOFFREY My dear Annys, this is neither the time nor place for you and me to argue out the matter. I must ask you to trust to my judgment.

ANNYS I can understand your refusing, but why do you object to my -

GEOFFREY Because I do not choose for my wife's name to be linked with a movement that I regard as criminal. I forbid it.

[It was the moment that was bound to come. The man's instincts, training, have involuntarily asserted themselves. Shall the woman yield? If so, then down goes the whole movement—her claim to freedom of judgment, of action, in all things. All watch the struggle with breathless interest.]

ANNYS [She speaks very slowly, very quietly, but with a new note in her voice.] I am sorry, but I have given much thought to this matter, and—I do not agree with you.

MRS. PEEKIN You will help us?

ANNYS I will do what I can.

PEEKIN [He takes from his pocket a folded paper.] It is always so much more satisfactory when these things are in writing. Candidates, with the best intentions in the world, are apt to forget. [He has spread the paper on a corner of the table. He has in his hand his fountain-pen.]

ANNYS [With a smile.] I am not likely to forget, but if you wish it—[She approaches the table.]

GEOFFREY [He interposes. His voice is very low, almost a whisper.] My wife will not sign.

ANNYS [She also speaks low, but there is no yielding in her voice.] I am not only your wife. I have a duty also to others.

GEOFFREY It is for you to choose. [He leaves the way open to her.]

[The silence can almost be felt. She moves to the table, takes up the paper. It contains but a few lines of writing. Having read it, she holds out her hand for the pen. PEEKIN puts it in her hand. With a firm hand she signs, folds the paper, and returns it to him. She remains standing by the table. With the removal of the tension there comes a rustle, a breaking of the silence.]

MISS RICKETTS [She seizes ANNYS's hand, hanging listlessly by her side, and, stooping, kisses it.]

MISS BORLASSE That is all, isn't it?

PEEKIN We thank you, Mrs. Chilvers. Good afternoon.

ANNYS [The natural reaction is asserting itself. She pulls herself together sufficiently to murmur her answer.] Good afternoon.

MRS. PEEKIN [The DEPUTATION is moving away; she takes from her waist a small bunch of flowers, and, turning, places them in ANNYS'S hand.]

ANNYS [She smiles, remains standing silent, the flowers in her hand.]

["Good afternoons" are exchanged with some of the others. Finally:]

PEEKIN Good afternoon, Mr. Chilvers.

GEOFFREY [Who has moved away.] Good afternoon.

[The DEPUTATION joins SIGSBY by the door. He leads them out.]

ELIZABETH [To PHOEBE.] Are you going my way?

PHOEBE [She glances round at ANNYS.] Yes, I'll come with you.

ST. HERBERT I will put you into a bus, if you will let me. We don't sport many cabs in East Poplar. [He is helping ELIZABETH with her cloak.]

ELIZABETH Thank you.

LAMB I've got to go up West. [To GEOFFREY.] Will you be at the House this evening?

GEOFFREY [He is standing by the desk pretending to look at some papers]. I shall look in about ten o'clock.

LAMB One or two things I want to say to you. Goodbye for the present.

GEOFFREY Goodbye!

PHOEBE Goodbye, old man. [She stretches out her hand.]

GEOFFREY Goodbye. [She shakes hands with a smile, exchanges a casual "goodbye" with ELIZABETH.]

[They go towards the door.]

[SIGSBY re-enters.]

SIGSBY [To LAMB.] Are you going?

LAMB Yes. I'll see you to-morrow morning. About ten o'clock.

SIGSBY I shall be here. [He exchanges a "good afternoon" with the others.]

[They go out. SIGSBY crosses and goes into the other room.]

ANNYS [She has let fall the flowers on the table. She crosses to where GEOFFREY still stands by the desk, his back towards her. She stretches out her hand, touches him. He does not move.] Geoffrey!

[But still he takes no notice.]

I am so sorry. We must talk it over quietly—at home.

GEOFFREY [He turns.] Home! I have no home. I have neither children nor wife. I KEEP a political opponent.

[ANNYS starts back with a cry. He crosses in front of her and seats himself at the table. The flowers are lying there; he throws them into the waste-paper basket.]

ANNYS [She puts on her cloak, moves towards the door. Half-way she pauses, makes a movement towards him. But he will not see. Then a hard look comes into her eyes, and without another word she goes out, leaving the door open.]

[SIGSBY is heard moving in the other room.]

GEOFFREY [He is writing.] Sigsby.

SIGSBY Hallo!

GEOFFREY That poster I told young Gordon I wouldn't sanction, "The Woman spouting politics, the Man returning to a slattern's home."

[SIGSBY enters.]

SIGSBY I have countermanded them.

GEOFFREY Countermand them again. We shall want a thousand.

SIGSBY [Can hardly believe his ears.]

GEOFFREY [With a gesture round the room.] All of them. "A Man for Men!" "Save the Children!" "Guard your Homes!" All the damned collection. Order as many as you want.

SIGSBY [His excitement rising.] I can go ahead. You mean it?

GEOFFREY [He looks at him.] It's got to be a fight! [A moment. He returns to his writing.] Telephone Hake that I shall be dining at the Reform Club.

CURTAIN.

THE THIRD ACT

SCENE:- A room in the Town Hall, Poplar. A high, bare, cold room, unfurnished except for cane-bottomed chairs ranged against the walls. French windows right give on to a balcony overlooking the street. Door in back opens upon a stone passage. A larger door opens into another room, through which one passes to reach the room in which the counting of the votes is taking place. A fire burns— or rather tries to burn. The room is lighted from the centre of the ceiling by an electric sun. A row of hat-pegs is on the wall between the two doors. The time is about 9 p.m.

[People entering from the street wear coats or cloaks, &c., the season being early spring. If passing through or staying in the room, they take off their outdoor things and hang them up, putting them on again before going out.]

[JAWBONES is coaxing the reluctant fire by using a newspaper as a blower. He curses steadily under his breath. The door opens. GINGER enters; she is dressed in cheap furs.]

JAWBONES Shut the door, can't yer!

GINGER Don't yer want a draught?

JAWBONES No, I don't. Not any more than I've got.

GINGER [She shuts the door.] 'Ave they begun counting the votes?

JAWBONES Been at it for the last three-quarters of an hour.

GINGER Who's going to win?

JAWBONES One of 'em.

[LADY MOGTON has entered. She has come from the room where they are counting the votes.]

Shut that door! [He glances over his shoulder, sees his mistake.] Beg pardon! [To himself.] Thought 'twas the other fool!

LADY MOGTON [She shuts the door. To GINGER.] Have you seen Mrs. Chilvers?

GINGER Not since the afternoon, your ladyship.

LADY MOGTON She is coming, I suppose?

GINGER I think so, your ladyship.

LADY MOGTON It's very cold in here, Gordon.

JAWBONES Yes, my lady. Not what I call a cosy room.

LADY MOGTON [To GINGER.] Jump into a cab. See if you can find her. Perhaps she has been detained at one of the committee-rooms. Tell her she ought to be here.

GINGER Yes, your ladyship. [She crosses, opens door.]

JAWBONES Shut the door.

GINGER Oh, shut -

[She finds herself face to face with a MESSENGER carrying a ballot- box.]

I beg yer pardon! [She goes out, closes door.]

LADY MOGTON [To the MESSENGER.] Is that the last?

MESSENGER Generally is. Isle of Dogs!

[He goes into the other room.]

LADY MOGTON [To JAWBONES.] Do you know where Mr. Chilvers is?

[There comes a bloodthirsty yell from the crowd outside.]

JAWBONES Not unless that's 'im. [He finishes for the time being with the fire. Rises.]

[JANET enters.]

LADY MOGTON Was that you they were yelling at?

JANET No, it's Mr. Sigsby.

[Another yell is heard. Out of it a shrill female voice—
"Mind 'is fice; yer spoiling it!"]

The Woman's Laundry Union have taken such a strong
dislike to him.

[A final yell. Then a voice: "That's taken some of the
starch out of him!" followed by a shriek of laughter.]

JAWBONES 'E only suggested as 'ow there was enough
old washerwomen in Parliament as it was.

LADY MOGTON A most unnecessary remark. It will
teach him -

[SIGSBY enters, damaged. His appearance is comic.
LADY MOGTON makes no effort to repress a grim
smile.]

SIGSBY Funny, ain't it?

LADY MOGTON I am sorry.

SIGSBY [He snarls.] "The Mother's Hand shall Help
Us!" One of your posters, I think.

LADY MOGTON You shouldn't have insulted them—
calling them old washerwomen!

SIGSBY Insult! Can't one indulge in a harmless jeu d'esprit—[he pronounces it according to his own ideas]—without having one's clothes torn off one's back? [Fiercely.] What do you mean by it— disgracing your sex?

LADY MOGTON Are you addressing me?

SIGSBY All of you. Upsetting the foundations upon which society has been reared—the natural and lawful subjection of the woman to the man. Why don't you read St. Paul?

LADY MOGTON St. Paul was addressing Christians. When men behave like Christians there will be no need of Votes for Women. You read St. Paul on men. [To JANET.] I shall want you!

[She goes out, followed by JANET.]

[SIGSBY gives vent to a gesture.]

JAWBONES Getting saucy, ain't they?

SIGSBY Over-indulgence. That's what the modern woman is suffering from. Gets an idea on Monday that she'd like the whole world altered; if it isn't done by Saturday, raises hell! Where's the guv'nor?

JAWBONES Hasn't been here.

SIGSBY [Hands JAWBONES his damaged hat.] See if they can do anything to that. If not, get me a new one. [He forks out a sovereign.] Sure to be some shops open in the High Street. [LAMB and ST. HERBERT enter.]

LAMB Hallo! have they been mauling you?

SIGSBY [He snatches the damaged hat from JAWBONES, to hand it back the next moment; holds it out.] Woman's contribution to politics. Get me a collar at the same time—sixteen and a half.

[JAWBONES takes his cap and goes out. The men hang up their overcoats.]

SIGSBY Where's it all going to end? That's what I want to know!

ST. HERBERT Where most things end. In the millennium, according to its advocates. In the ruin of the country, according to its opponents. In mild surprise on the part of the next generation that ever there was any fuss about it.

SIGSBY In amazement, you mean, that their fathers were so blind as not to see where it was leading. My boy, this is going to alter the whole relationship between the sexes!

ST. HERBERT Is it so perfect as it is?

[A silence.]

Might it not be established on a more workable, a more enduring basis if woman were allowed a share in the shaping of it?

[Some woman in the crowd starts the refrain, "We'll hang old Asquith on a sour apple tree." It is taken up with quiet earnestness by others.]

SIGSBY Shaping it! Nice sort of shape it will be by the time that lot [with a gesture, including the crowd, LADY MOGTON & Co.] have done knocking it about. Wouldn't be any next generation to be surprised at anything if some of them had their way.

ST. HERBERT The housebreakers come first—not a class of work demanding much intelligence; the builders come later. Have you seen Chilvers?

LAMB I left him at the House. He couldn't get away.

SIGSBY There's your object-lesson for you. We don't need to go far. A man's whole career ruined by the wife he nourishes.

ST. HERBERT How do you mean, "ruined?"

SIGSBY So it is. If she wins the election and claims the seat. Do you think the Cabinet will want him? Their latest addition compelled to appeal to the House of

Commons to fight for him against his own womenfolk. [Grunts.] He'll be the laughing-stock of the whole country.

ST. HERBERT Do you know for certain that they mean to claim the seat?

SIGSBY "Wait and see" is their answer.

LAMB Hasn't Chilvers any idea?

SIGSBY Can't get him to talk. Don't think he's seen her since that shindy over the Deputation.

LAMB Humph!

SIGSBY Even if she herself wished to draw back, the others would overrule her.

LAMB I'm not so sure of that. She's got a way of shutting her mouth that reminds me of my old woman.

SIGSBY The arrangement, as he explained it to me, was that the whole thing was to end with the polling. It was to have been a mere joke, a mere ballon d'essai. The mistake he made was thinking he could depend on her.

LAMB Guess she made the same mistake. You can fight and shake hands afterwards; it doesn't go with kissing.

SIGSBY Man and woman were not made to fight. It was never intended.

[The woman's "Marseillaise" has been taken up by the crowd. The chorus has been reached.]

Oh, damn your row! [He slams to the window; it was ajar.]

[JAWBONES has entered, with his purchases.]

[Turning from window he sees JAWBONES, goes to meet him.] Couldn't they do anything?

JAWBONES [He has bought a new hat; has also brought back the remains. He shakes his head.] No good for anything else but a memento.

SIGSBY [With a grunt he snatches the thing and flings it into a corner. Tries on the new one.]

JAWBONES 'Ow's it feel?

[SIGSBY, with the help of JAWBONES, attends to his appearance.]

LAMB [To ST. HERBERT.] No use talking to her, I suppose?

ST. HERBERT [Shrugs his shoulders.] She'll do what she imagines to be her duty. Women are so uncivilised.

[A burst of cheering is heard. A shrill male voice: "Three cheers for Winston Churchill!" It is followed by an explosion of yells.]

ST. HERBERT Who's that?

LAMB [He has opened the window.] Phoebe Mogton!

SIGSBY What a family!

[JANET has entered.]

JANET Is that Mrs. Chilvers? [To LAMB and ST. HERBERT.] Good evening.

ST. HERBERT Good evening.

LAMB No; it's her sister.

JANET I wonder she doesn't come.

SIGSBY What are the latest figures? Do you know?

[PHOEBE enters.]

JANET I forget the numbers. Mrs. Chilvers is forty ahead.

PHOEBE Forty ahead! [To JANET.] Did you order the band?

LAMB [To SIGSBY.] The Dock division was against him to a man; that Shipping Bill has upset them.

JANET No. I didn't think we should want the band.

PHOEBE Not want it! My dear girl -

JANET Perhaps Lady Mogton has ordered it, I'll ask her. [She goes out.]

SIGSBY Hadn't you better "Wait and see"? It isn't over yet.

PHOEBE We may as well have it! It can play the Dead March   in
"Saul" if you win. [She laughs.]

SIGSBY [Grunts. To LAMB.] Are you coming?

[He goes out.]

LAMB Yes. [To ST. HERBERT.] Are you coming?

ST. HERBERT Hardly worth while; nearly over, isn't it?

LAMB It generally takes an hour and a half. [He looks at his watch.] Another forty minutes. Perhaps less. [He goes out.]

PHOEBE I do love to make him ratty. Wish it wasn't poor old Geoff we were fighting.

ST. HERBERT When I marry, it will be the womanly woman.

PHOEBE No chance for me then?

ST. HERBERT I don't say that. I can see you taking your political opinions from your husband, and thinking them your own.

PHOEBE Good heavens!

ST. HERBERT The brainy woman will think for herself. And then I foresee some lively breakfast tables.

PHOEBE Humph! No fear, I suppose, of a man taking his views from his wife and thinking them his own?

ST. HERBERT That may be the solution. The brainy woman will have to marry the manly man.

[GINGER enters.]

JAWBONES [He is on his knees blowing the fire. In a low growl.] Shut the door!

GINGER Can't till I'm inside, can I? [Shuts it.] Where's Lady Mogton?

JAWBONES I don't know.

PHOEBE What do you want her for?

GINGER Only to tell her that I can't find Chilvers.

PHOEBE Isn't she here?

GINGER Not unless she's come while I've been out.

[JANET enters.]

JANET Oh, Lady Mogton -

PHOEBE [Interrupting her.] Isn't Annys here?

JANET No. [To GINGER.] Haven't you found her?

GINGER [Shakes her head.] Been everywhere I could think of.

PHOEBE [To herself.] She couldn't have gone home? Is there a telephone here?

JANET The room's locked up.

JAWBONES There's one at 118, High Street. Shall I go, miss?

PHOEBE No, thanks. I'll go myself. Oh, what about the band?

JANET Lady Mogton says she'd like it. If it isn't too tired.

GINGER It's at Sell's Coffee-'ouse in Piggott Street. I 'eard them practising.

PHOEBE Good. I shan't be more than a few minutes.

ST. HERBERT I'll come with you, if I may? I've got some news that may be of use to you.

PHOEBE Do. [To GINGER.] Stop here, I may want you.

[PHOEBE and ST. HERBERT go out.]

JANET How was Mrs. Chilvers seeming this afternoon?

GINGER Never 'eard 'er speak better, miss.

JANET Did you stop to the end?

GINGER Not quite. Mrs. Spender wanted some shopping done.

[JANET goes out.]

GINGER Can I 'elp yer?

JAWBONES Yer might hold the piper while I blow.

[The fire begins to burn.]

GINGER It's getting brighter.

JAWBONES That's caught it.

GINGER Wonderful what a little coaxing will do.

JAWBONES [He is still squatting on his heels, folding up the paper. He looks up.] Ain't yer ever thought of that, instead of worrying about the vote?

GINGER [She moves away.] You don't understand us wimmin.

JAWBONES [He has risen. He pauses in his folding of the paper.] Don't say that.

GINGER Why should we coax yer—for our rights?

JAWBONES Because it's the easiest way of getting 'em.

GINGER [She has become oratorical.] Our appeal is not to man [with upraised hand] but to Justice!

JAWBONES Oh! And what does the lidy say?

GINGER [Descending.] 'Ow do yer mean?

JAWBONES To your appeal. Is she goin' to give 'em to yer ? You tike my tip: if yer in a 'urry, you get a bit on account—from Man. 'Ere. [He dives into his pocket, produces, wrapped up in tissue paper, a ring, which he exhibits to her.] That's a bit more in your line.

GINGER [Her eyes sparkle. She takes the ring in her hand. Then problems come to her.] Why do yer want me, William?

JAWBONES Because, in spite of all, I love yer.

GINGER [She looks into the future.] What will I be? A general servant, without wages.

JAWBONES The question, as it seems to me, is, which of us two is the biggest fool? Instead of thirty bob a week in my pocket to spend as I like—guess I'll 'ave to be content with three 'alf- crowns.

GINGER Seven an' six! Rather a lot, Bill, out o' thirty bob. Don't leave much for me an' the children.

JAWBONES I shall 'ave to get my dinners.

GINGER I could mike yer somethin' tasty to tike with yer. Then with, say—three shillings -

JAWBONES 'Ere—[He is on the point of snatching back the ring. He encounters her eyes. There is a moment's battle. The Eternal Feminine conquers.] Will yer always look as sweet as yer do now?

GINGER Always, Bill. So long as yer good to me!

[She slips the ring over her finger, still with her eyes drawing him. He catches her to him in fierce passion, kisses her.]

[A loud shrill female cheer comes from the crowd. The cheer is renewed and renewed.]

JAWBONES [He breaks away and goes to the window.] 'Ullo! What are they shoutin' about now? [He looks out.] It's the Donah!

GINGER Mrs. Chilvers?

JAWBONES Yus. Better not get wearin' it—may shock their feelings.

GINGER [She gazes rapturously at the ring as she draws it off.] It is a beauty! I do love yer, Bill.

[There enter ANNYS and ELIZABETH. ANNYS is excited; she is laughing and talking.]

ANNYS [Laughing while she rearranges her hat and hair.] A little embarrassing. That red-haired girl—she carried me right up the steps. I was afraid she would -

[JAWBONES has been quick enough to swing a chair into place just in time to receive her.]

[She recovers herself.] Thank you.

ELIZABETH [She hands ANNYS a smelling-bottle. To JAWBONES.] Open the window a few inches.

[He does so. Some woman, much interrupted, is making a speech.]

[JANET opens the door a little way and looks in.]

JANET Oh, it is you! I am glad!

[She goes out again.]

ELIZABETH Are the others all here?

GINGER 'Er ladyship is watching the counting. Miss Phoebe 'as just gone out -

[PHOEBE enters.]

Oh, 'ere she is.

PHOEBE Hullo! [She is taking off her things.] Wherever have you been? We've been scouring the neighbourhood -

[LADY MOGTON enters, followed by JANET.]

I say, you're looking jolly chippy.

ELIZABETH We had an extra enthusiastic meeting. She spoke for rather a long time. I made her come home with me and lie down. I think she is all right now.

LADY MOGTON Would you like to see a doctor?

PHOEBE There is a very good man close here. [She turns to JAWBONES, who is still near the window.] Gordon -

ANNYS [Interrupting.] No. Please don't. I am quite all right. I hate strange doctors.

PHOEBE Well, let me send for Whitby; he could be here in twenty minutes.

ANNYS I wish you would all leave me alone. There's absolutely nothing to fuss about whatever. We pampered women—we can't breathe the same air that ordinary mortals have to. We ought to be ashamed of ourselves.

PHOEBE [To herself.] Obstinate pig.

[She catches JAWBONES' eye; unnoticed by the others, she takes him aside. They whisper.]

ANNYS How is it going?

LADY MOGTON You must be prepared for winning. [She puts again the question that ANNYS has frequently been asked to answer during the last few days.] What are you going to do?

[MRS. MOUNTCALM-VILLIERS enters, as usual in a flutter of excitement.]

MRS. MOUNTCALM-VILLIERS Am I late?

[They brush her back into silence. ELIZABETH takes charge of her.]

ANNYS [She has risen.] You think it wise tactics, to make it impossible for Geoffrey to be anything else in the future but our enemy?

LADY MOGTON [Contemptuously.] You are thinking of him, and not of the cause.

ANNYS And if I were! Haven't I made sacrifice enough?—more than any of you will ever know. Ay—and would make more, if I felt it was demanded of me. I don't! [Her burst of anger is finished. She turns, smiling.] I'm much more cunning than you think. There will be other elections we shall want to fight. With the Under- Secretary for Home Affairs in sympathy with us, the Government will find it difficult to interfere. Don't you see how clever I am?

[JAWBONES, having received his instructions from PHOEBE, has slipped out unobserved. He has beckoned to GINGER; she has followed him. PHOEBE has joined the group.]

MRS. MOUNTCALM-VILLIERS. There's something in that.

JANET Is Mr. Chilvers still in sympathy with us?

PHOEBE Of course he is. A bit rubbed up the wrong way just at present; that's our fault. When Annys goes down, early next mouth, to fight the Exchange Division of Manchester, we shall have him with us.

[A moment.]

LADY MOGTON Where do you get that from?

PHOEBE From St. Herbert. The present member is his cousin. They say he can't live more than a week.

MRS. MOUNTCALM-VILLIERS It really seems like Providence.

ANNYS [Has taken the opportunity of giving PHOEBE a grateful squeeze of the hand.].

LADY MOGTON You will fight Manchester?

ANNYS Yes. [Laughs.] And make myself a public nuisance if I win.

LADY MOGTON Well, must be content with that, I suppose. Better not come in; the room's rather crowded. I'll keep you informed how things are going.

[She goes out, followed by JANET.]

MRS. MOUNTCALM-VILLIERS I'll stay with you, dear.

PHOEBE I want you to come and be photographed for the Daily Mirror. The man's waiting downstairs.

ELIZABETH I'll stop with Annys.

MRS. MOUNTCALM-VILLIERS I'm not quite sure, you know, that I take well by flashlight.

PHOEBE You wait till you've seen mamma! We must have you. They want you for the centre of the page.

MRS. MOUNTCALM-VILLIERS Well, if it's really -

PHOEBE [To the others.] Shall see you again. [She winks. Then to MRS. MOUNTCALM-VILLIERS.] We mustn't keep them waiting. They are giving us a whole page.

[PHOEBE takes MRS. MOUNTCALM-VILLIERS out. ELIZABETH has followed to the door; she closes it. ANNYS has reseated herself, facing the fire.]

ELIZABETH When did you see your husband last?

ANNYS Not since—Tuesday, wasn't it, that we went round to his rooms. Why?

ELIZABETH I'm thinking about Manchester. What was it he said to you?

ANNYS Oh, we were, both of us, a little over-excited, I suppose. He has—[she hesitates, finally answers]—he has always been so eager for children.

ELIZABETH Yes. So many men are; not having to bear the pain and inconvenience themselves.

ANNYS Oh, well, they have to provide for them when they do come. That's fair enough division, I su-[Suddenly she turns fiercely.] Why do you talk like that? As if we women were cowards. Do you think if God sent me a child I should grudge Him the price!

ELIZABETH Do you want Him to?

ANNYS I don't know; prayed Him to, once.

ELIZABETH [She lays her hand upon her.] It isn't a few more mothers that the world has need of. It is the women whom God has appointed—to whom He has given freedom, that they may champion the cause of the mothers, helpless by reason of their motherhood.

[A moment. GEOFFREY enters.]

GEOFFREY Good evening.

ANNYS [Rises; a smile struggles for possession. But he only shakes hands, and it dies away.]

ELIZABETH Good evening.

[They shake hands.]

GEOFFREY You are not interested in the counting?

ANNYS The room is rather crowded. Mamma thought I would be better out here. How have you been?

GEOFFREY Oh, all right. It's going to be a very near thing, they tell me.

ANNYS Yes, I shall be glad when it's over.

GEOFFREY It's always a trying time. What are you going to do, if you win?

[LADY MOGTON looks in.]

LADY MOGTON [Seeing GEOFFREY.] Oh, good evening.

GEOFFREY Good evening.

LADY MOGTON Chilvers, 2,960—Annys Chilvers, 2,874. [She disappears—closes door.]

ANNYS Perhaps I'm not going to win. [She goes to him, smiling.] I hope you'll win. I would so much rather you won.

GEOFFREY Very kind of you. I'm afraid that won't make it a certainty.

ANNYS [His answer has hardened her again.] How can I? It would not be fair. Without your consent I should never have entered upon it. It was understood that the seat, in any case, would be yours.

GEOFFREY I would rather you considered yourself quite free. In warfare it doesn't pay to be "fair" to one's enemy.

ANNYS [Still hardening.] Besides, there is no need. There will be other opportunities. I can contest some other constituency. If I win, claim the seat for that.

[A moment.]

GEOFFREY So this is only the beginning? You have decided to devote yourself to a political career?

ANNYS Why not?

GEOFFREY If I were to ask you to abandon it, to come back to your place at my side—helping me, strengthening me?

ANNYS You mean you would have me abandon my own task—merge myself in you?

GEOFFREY Be my wife.

ANNYS It would not be right. I, too, have my work.

GEOFFREY If it takes you away from me?

ANNYS Why need it take me away from you? Why cannot we work together for common ends, each in our own way?

GEOFFREY We talked like that before we tried it. Marriage is not a partnership; it is a leadership.

ANNYS [She looks at him.] You mean—an ownership.

GEOFFREY Perhaps you're right. I didn't make it. I'm only— beginning to understand it.

ANNYS And I too. It is not what I want.

GEOFFREY You mean its duties have become irksome to you.

ANNYS I mean I want to be the judge myself of what are my duties.

GEOFFREY I no longer count. You will go your way without me?

ANNYS I must go the way I think right.

GEOFFREY [He flings away.] If you win to-night you will do well to make the most of it. Take my advice and claim the seat.

ANNYS [Looks at him puzzled.]

ELIZABETH Why?

GEOFFREY Because [with a short, ugly laugh] the Lord only knows when you'll get another opportunity.

ELIZABETH You are going to stop us?

GEOFFREY To stop women from going to the poll. The Bill will be introduced on Monday. Carried through all its stages the same week.

ELIZABETH You think it will pass?

GEOFFREY The Whips assure me that it will.

ANNYS But they cannot, they dare not, without your assent. The— [The light breaks in upon her.] Who is bringing it in?

GEOFFREY I am.

ANNYS [Is going to speak.]

GEOFFREY [He stops her.] Oh, I'm prepared for all that—ridicule, abuse. "Chilvers's Bill for the Better Regulation of Mrs. Chilvers," they'll call it. I can hear their laughter. Yours won't be among it.

ANNYS But, Geoffrey! What is the meaning? Merely to spite me, are you going to betray a cause that you have professed belief in— that you have fought for?

GEOFFREY Yes—if it is going to take you away from me. I want you. No, I don't want a friend—"a fellow-worker"—some interesting rival in well doing. I can get all that outside my home. I want a wife. I want the woman I love to belong to me—to be mine. I am not troubling about being up to date; I'm talking what I feel—what every male creature must have felt since the protoplasmic cell developed instincts. I want a woman to love—a woman to work for—a woman to fight for—a woman to be a slave to. But mine—mine, and nothing else. All the rest [he makes a gesture] is talk.

[He closes the window, shutting out the hubbub of the crowd.]

ANNYS [A strange, new light has stolen in. She is bewildered, groping.] But—all this is new between us. You have not talked like this for—not since— We were just good friends—comrades.

GEOFFREY And might have remained so, God knows! I suppose we're made like that. So long as there was no danger passion slept. I cannot explain it. I only know that now, beside the thought of losing you, all else in the world seems meaningless. The Woman's Movement! [He makes a gesture of contempt.] Men have wrecked kingdoms for a woman before now—and will again. I want you! [He comes to her.] Won't you come back to me, that we may build up the home we used to dream of? Wasn't the old love good? What has this new love to give you? Work that man can do better. The cause of the women—the children! Has woman loved woman better than man? Will the world be better for the children, man and woman contending? Come back to me. Help me. Help me to fight for all good women. Teach me how I may make the world better—for our children.

ANNYS [The light is in her eyes. She stands a moment. Her hands are going out to him.]

ELIZABETH [She comes between them.] Yes, go to him. He will be very good to you. Good men are kind to women, kind even to their dogs. You will be among the pampered few! You will be happy. And the others! What does it matter?

[They draw apart. She stands between them, the incarnation of the spirit of sex war.]

The women that have not kind owners—the dogs that have not kind masters—the dumb women, chained to their endless, unpaid drudgery! Let them be content. What are they but man's chattel? To be honoured if it pleases him, or to be cast into the dust. Man's pauper! Bound by his laws, subject to his whim; her every hope, her every aspiration, owed to his charity. She toils for him without ceasing: it should be her "pleasure." She bears him children, when he chooses to desire them. They are his to do as he will by. Why seek to change it? Our man is kind. What have they to do with us: the women beaten, driven, overtasked—the women without hope or joy, the livers of grey lives that men may laugh and spend—the women degraded lower than the beasts to pander to the beast in man—the women outraged and abandoned, bearing to the grave the burden of man's lust? Let them go their way. They are but our sisters of sorrow. And we who could help them—we to whom God has given the weapons: the brain, and the courage—we make answer: "I have married a husband, and I cannot come."

[A silence.]

GEOFFREY Well, you have heard. [He makes a gesture.] What is your answer?

ANNYS [She comes to him.] Don't you love me enough to humour me a little—to put up with my vexing ways? I so want to help, to feel I am doing just a little, to make the world kinder. I know you can do it better, but I want so to be "in it." [She laughs.] Let us forget all this. Wake up to-morrow morning with fresh hearts. You will be Member for East Poplar. And then you shall help me to win Manchester. [She puts her hands upon his breast: she would have him take her in his arms.] I am not strong enough to fight alone.

GEOFFREY I want you. Let Manchester find some one else.

ANNYS [She draws away from him.] And if I cannot— will not?

GEOFFREY I bring in my Bill on Monday. We'll be quite frank about it. That is my price—you. I want you!

ANNYS You mean it comes to that: a whole cause dependent on a man and a woman!

GEOFFREY Yes, that is how the world is built. On each man and woman. "How does it shape my life, my hopes?" So will each make answer.

[LADY MOGTON enters. She stands silent.]

ELIZABETH Is it over?

LADY MOGTON Annys Chilvers, 3,604—Geoffrey Chilvers, 3,590.

[JANET enters.]

JANET [She rushes to ANNYS, embraces her.] You've won, you've won! [She flies to the window, opens it, and goes out on to the balcony.]

[PHOEBE enters, followed by MRS. MOUNTCALM-VILLIERS.]

PHOEBE Is it true?

LADY MOGTON Pretty close. Majority of 14.

MRS. MOUNTCALM-VILLIERS For us?

LADY MOGTON For us.

[JANET by this time has announced the figures. There is heard a great burst of cheering, renewed again and again.]

JANET [Re-entering.] They want you! They want you!

[Mingled with the cheering come cries of "Speech! Speech!"]

LADY MOGTON You must say something.

[The band strikes up "The Conquering Hero." The women crowd round ANNYS, congratulating her. GEOFFREY stands apart.]

PHOEBE [Screaming above the din.] Put on your cloak.

JANET [Rushes and gets it.]

[They wrap it round her.]

[ANNYS goes out on to the balcony, followed by the other women. ELIZABETH, going last, fires a parting smile of triumph at GEOFFREY.]

[A renewed burst of cheering announces their arrival on the balcony. The crowd bursts into "For She's a Jolly Good Fellow"— the band, making a quick change, joins in. GEOFFREY remains centre.]

[JAWBONES enters unobserved. The singing ends with three cheers. ANNYS is speaking. GEOFFREY turns and sees JAWBONES.]

GEOFFREY [With a smile.] Give me down my coat, will you?

JAWBONES [He is sympathetic. He helps him on with it.] Shall I get you a cab, sir?

GEOFFREY No, thanks. I'll pick one up. [He goes towards the door, then stops.] Is there any other way out—not through the main entrance?

JAWBONES Yes, sir. There's a side door opening on Woodstock Road. I'll show it you.

GEOFFREY Thanks. [He follows JAWBONES out.]

[A burst of cheering comes from the crowd.]

CURTAIN.

THE FOURTH ACT

SCENE:- Russell Square. The morning-room [on the ground floor]. A small, cheerful room, furnished in Chippendale, white panelled, with Adams fireplace in which a bright fire is burning. Two deep easy-chairs are before the fire. The window-curtains of red damask are drawn. An oval table occupies the centre of the room. The door at back opens upon the hall. Only one light burns, an electric lamp on a table just above the fire.

TIME:- Midnight.

[The door opens. GEOFFREY enters. He has left his out-door things in the hall. He crosses and rings the bell. A moment.]

[HAKE enters.]

GEOFFREY Oh, you, Hake! There wasn't any need for you to have stopped.

HAKE I was not sure of your arrangements. I thought perhaps I might be wanted.

GEOFFREY Sorry. I ought to have told you.

HAKE It's been no inconvenience, sir. I told Mrs. Hake not to sit up.

GEOFFREY [He is opening and reading his letters left for him on the table.] Does she generally sit up for you?

HAKE As a rule, sir. We like a little chat before going to bed.

GEOFFREY [His eyes on a letter.] What do you find to chat about?

HAKE Oh, there is so much for a husband and wife to talk about. The— As a rule.

[A clock on the mantelpiece strikes one.]

GEOFFREY What's that?

HAKE Quarter past twelve, sir.

GEOFFREY Has your mistress come in?

HAKE Not yet, sir. Has the election gone all right, sir?

GEOFFREY For Mrs. Chilvers, yes. She is now member for East Poplar.

HAKE I am sorry. It has been a great surprise to me.

GEOFFREY The result?

HAKE The whole thing, sir. Such a sweet lady, we all thought her.

GEOFFREY Life, Hake, is a surprising affair.

[A ring is heard.]

I expect that's she. She has forgotten her key.

[HAKE goes out.]

[GEOFFREY continues his letters. A few moments pass; HAKE re- enters, closes the door.]

HAKE [He seems puzzled.] It's a lady, sir

[GEOFFREY turns.]

HAKE At least—hardly a lady. A Mrs. Chinn.

GEOFFREY Mrs. Chinn! [He glances at his watch.] At twelve o'clock at night. Well, all right. I'll see her.

[HAKE opens the door, speaks to MRS. CHINN. She enters, in bonnet and shawl.]

HAKE Mrs. Chinn.

GEOFFREY Good evening, Mrs. Chinn.

MRS. CHINN Good evening, sir.

GEOFFREY You needn't stop, Hake. I shan't be wanting anything.

HAKE Thank you.

GEOFFREY Apologise for me to Mrs. Hake. Good-night.

HAKE Good-night, sir.

[HAKE goes out. A minute later the front door is heard to slam.]

GEOFFREY Won't you sit down? [He puts a chair for her left of the table.]

MRS. CHINN [Seating herself.] Thank you, sir.

GEOFFREY [He half sits on the arm of the easy-chair below the fire.] What's the trouble?

MRS. CHINN It's my boy, sir—my youngest. He's been taking money that didn't belong to him.

GEOFFREY Um. Has it been going on for long?

MRS. CHINN About six months, sir. I only heard of it to-night. You see, his wife died a year ago. She was such a good manager. And after she was gone he seems to have got into debt.

GEOFFREY What were his wages?

MRS. CHINN Nineteen shillings a week, sir. And that with the rent and three young children—well, it wants thinking out.

GEOFFREY From whom did he take the money—his employers?

MRS. CHINN Yes, sir. He was the carman. They had always trusted him to collect the accounts.

GEOFFREY How much, would you say, was the defalcation?

MRS. CHINN I beg pardon, sir.

GEOFFREY How much does it amount to, the sums that he has taken?

MRS. CHINN Six pounds, sir, Mr. Cohen says it comes to.

GEOFFREY Won't they accept repayment?

MRS. CHINN Yes, sir. Mr. Cohen has been very nice about it. He is going to let me pay it off by instalments.

GEOFFREY Well, then, that gets over most of the trouble.

MRS. CHINN Well, you see, sir, unfortunately, Mr. Cohen gave information to the police the moment he discovered it.

GEOFFREY Umph! Can't he say he made a mistake?

MRS. CHINN They say it must go for trial, sir. That he can only withdraw the charge in court.

GEOFFREY Um!

MRS. CHINN You see, sir—a thing like that—[She recovers herself.] It clings to a lad.

GEOFFREY What do you want me to do?

MRS. CHINN Well, sir, I thought that, perhaps—you see, sir, he has got a brother in Canada who would help him; and I thought that if I could ship him off -

GEOFFREY You want me to tip the wink to the police to look the other way while you smuggle this young malefactor out of the clutches of the law?

MRS. CHINN [Quite indifferent to the moral aspect of the case.] If you would be so kind, sir.

GEOFFREY Umph! I suppose you know what you're doing; appealing through your womanhood to man's weakness—employing "backstairs influence" to gain your private ends, indifferent to the higher issues of the public weal? All the things that are going to cease when woman has the vote.

MRS. CHINN You see, sir, he's the youngest.

[Gradually the decent but dingy figure of MRS. CHINN has taken to itself new shape. To GEOFFREY, it almost seems as though there were growing out of the shadows over against him the figure of great Artemis herself— Artemis of the Thousand Breasts. He had returned home angry, bitter against all women. As she unfolds her simple tale understanding comes to him. So long as there are "Mrs. Chinns" in the world, Woman claims homage.]

GEOFFREY How many were there?

MRS. CHINN Ten altogether, six living.

GEOFFREY Been a bit of a struggle for you, hasn't it?

MRS. CHINN It has been a bit difficult, at times; especially after their poor father died.

GEOFFREY How many were you left with?

MRS. CHINN Eight, sir.

GEOFFREY How on earth did you manage to keep them?

MRS. CHINN Well, you see, sir, the two eldest, they were earning a little. I don't think I could have done it without that.

GEOFFREY Wasn't there any source from which you could have obtained help? What was your husband?

MRS. CHINN He worked in the shipyards, sir. There was some talk about it. But, of course, that always means taking the children away from you.

GEOFFREY Would not that have been better for them?

MRS. CHINN Not always, sir. Of course, if I hadn't been able to do my duty by them I should have had to. But, thank God, I've always been strong.

GEOFFREY [He rises.] I will see what can be done.

MRS. CHINN Thank you, sir.

GEOFFREY [Half-way, he turns.] When does the next boat sail—for Canada?

MRS. CHINN To-morrow night, sir, from Glasgow. I have booked his passage.

GEOFFREY [With a smile.] You seem to have taken everything for granted.

MRS. CHINN You see, sir, it's the disgrace. All the others are doing so well. It would upset them so.

[He goes out.]

[There is a moment.]

[ANNYS enters. She is wearing her outdoor things.]

ANNYS Mrs. Chinn!

MRS. CHINN [She has risen; she curtseys.] Good evening, ma'am.

ANNYS [She is taking off her hat.] Nothing wrong, is there?

MRS. CHINN My boy, ma'am, my youngest, has been getting into trouble.

ANNYS [She pauses, her hat in her hand.] They will, won't they? It's nothing serious, I hope?

MRS. CHINN I think it will be all right, ma'am, thanks to your good gentleman.

ANNYS [She lays aside her hat.] You have had a good many children, haven't you, Mrs. Chinn?

MRS. CHINN Ten altogether, ma'am; six living.

ANNYS Can one love ten, all at once?

[The cloak has fallen aside. MRS. CHINN is a much experienced lady.]

MRS. CHINN Just as many as come, dear. God sends the love with them.

[There is a moment; the two women are very close to one another. Then ANNYS gives a little cry and somehow their arms are round one another.]

[She mothers her into the easy chair above the fire; places a footstool under her feet.] You have your cry out, dearie, it will do you good.

ANNYS You look so strong and great.

MRS. CHINN It's the tears, dearie. [She arranges the foot-stool.]
You keep your feet up.

[The handle of the door is heard. MRS. CHINN is standing beside her own chair. She is putting back her handkerchief into her bag.]

[GEOFFREY re-enters.]

[ANNYS is hidden in the easy chair. He does not see her.]

GEOFFREY Well, Mrs. Chinn, an exhaustive search for the accused will be commenced—next week.

MRS. CHINN Thank you, sir.

GEOFFREY What about the children—are they going with him?

MRS. CHINN No, sir; I thought he would be better without them till everything is settled.

GEOFFREY Who is taking care of them—you?

MRS. CHINN Yes, sir.

GEOFFREY And the passage money—how much was that?

MRS. CHINN Four pound fifteen.

GEOFFREY Would you mind my coming in, as a friend?

MRS. CHINN Well, if you don't mind, I'd rather not. I've always done everything for the children myself. It's been a fad of mine.

GEOFFREY [He makes a gesture of despair.] You mothers! You're so greedy. [He holds out his hand, smiling.] Goodbye.

MRS. CHINN [She takes his hand in hers.] God bless you, sir. And your good lady.

GEOFFREY [As he takes her to the door.] How will you get home?

MRS. CHINN I can get the Underground from Gower Street, sir.

[They go out talking about last trains and leaving the door open. The next moment the front door is heard to slam.]

[GEOFFREY re-enters.]

[ANNYS has moved round, so that coming back into the room he finds her there.]

GEOFFREY How long have you been in?

[He closes the door.]

ANNYS Only a few minutes—while you were at the telephone. I had to rest for a little while. Dr. Whitby brought me back in his motor.

GEOFFREY Was he down there?

ANNYS Phoebe had sent for him. I had been taken a little giddy earlier in the day.

GEOFFREY [He grunts. He is fighting with his tenderness.] Don't wonder at it. All this overwork and excitement.

ANNYS I'm afraid I've been hurting you.

GEOFFREY [Still growling.] Both been hurting each other, I expect.

ANNYS [She smiles.] It's so easy to hurt those that love us.

[She makes a little movement, feebly stretches out her arms to him. Wondering, he comes across to her. She draws him down beside her, takes his arms and places them about her.] I want to feel that I belong to you. That you are strong. That I can rest upon you.

GEOFFREY [He cannot understand.] But only an hour ago—[He looks at her.] Have you, too, turned traitor to the Woman's Cause?

ANNYS [She answers smiling.] No. But woman, dear, is a much more complicated person than I thought her. It is only in this hour that God has revealed her to me. [She draws him closer.] I want you, dear—dear husband. Take care of us—both, won't you? I love you, I love you. I did not know how much.

GEOFFREY [He gathers her to him, kissing her, crooning over her.] Oh, my dear, my dear! My little one, my love, my wife!

ANNYS [She is laughing, crying.] But, Geoffrey, dear -

[He tries to calm her.]

No, let me. I want to— And then I'll be quite good, I promise— It's only fair to warn you. When I'm strong and can think again, I shall still want the vote. I shall want it more than ever.

GEOFFREY [He answers with a happy laugh, holding her in his arms.]

ANNYS You will help us? Because it's right, dear, isn't it? He will be my child as well as yours. You will let me help you make the world better for our child—and for all the children—and for all the mothers—and for all the dear, kind men: you will, won't you?

GEOFFREY I thought you were drifting away from me: that strange voices were calling you away from life and motherhood. God has laughed at my fears. He has sent you back to me with His command. We will fashion His world together, we two lovers, Man and Woman, joined together in all things. It is His will. His chains are the children's hands.

[Kneeling, he holds her in his arms.]

[THE CURTAIN FALLS.]

www.ingramcontent.com/pod-product-compliance
Lightning Source LLC
Chambersburg PA
CBHW021622270326
41931CB00008B/827